DO MORE DEALS

A Property Investors Guide to Finding More Deals, Raising More Money and Attracting More Opportunities

Tanner H. Hicks

Do More Deals
A Property Investors Guide to Finding More Deals, Raising More Money and Attracting More Opportunities

ISBN: 978-1-7385254-0-9 Paperback

Published by: Inspired By Publishing

Cover Designed By: Tanya Grant, The TNG Designs Group Limited

The strategies in this book are presented primarily for enjoyment and educational purposes. Every effort has been made to trace copyright holders and obtain their permission for the use of copyright material.

The information and resources provided in this book are based upon the authors' personal experiences. Any outcome, income statements or other results, are based on the authors' experiences and there is no guarantee that your experience will be the same. There is an inherent risk in any business enterprise or activity and there is no guarantee that you will have similar results as the author as a result of reading this book.

The author reserves the right to make changes and assumes no responsibility or liability whatsoever on behalf of any purchaser or reader of these materials.

TABLE OF CONTENTS

INTRODUCTION

In a world filled with the chaos of conflicting advice, information overload, false promises, and the uninterrupted barrage of marketing making us 'want more', there lies a hidden path for those brave enough to go after it.

Amidst this chaos, countless individuals deal with common challenges — whether that be an initial lack of clarity behind what they are trying to build, or a severe lack of confidence in themselves. I have spoken with, coached, and advised many people over the years, and it became clear to me that these struggles often prove to be the most testing obstacles they encounter.

This is because people always want more — more money, more time, more freedom, more flexibility, more choices. And whilst there is nothing wrong with that, often when drilled to provide a deeper reason as to why, that's usually as far as it goes.

What I see happening too often is that in the process of seeking 'more,' people are actually ending up with less — less money, less time, less freedom, less happiness.

They are somewhere down a rabbit hole, bashing their head against a brick wall because nothing seems to be working. I liken it to someone standing on the shores of a vast lake with a desire to reach the other side, where apparent lifestyles of luxury, opulence and uninterrupted happiness awaits.

These lifestyles also contain fulfilment, flexibility, choice, security, love — pretty much anything they don't yet have. They know they want to be over there, but they don't actually know exactly "where" on the other side of the lake they want to go.

What I see happening is that these folk look for the nearest boat and jump in. They push it out onto the water and hit go on the engine.

They believe, or rather, they have been conditioned to believe that simply being on that lake, in that boat, will lead them to success. Those constant messages from the world are telling them that success requires them to "just take that first step".

But what happens after a little time on the lake is that they start to question whether they are making any progress at all. They lose sight of where they have already come from. Or they wonder whether they are making enough progress for the amount of energy they are putting in. They start to question whether they were standing next to a lake in the first place or whether it was, in fact, an endless ocean.

Not only does it seemingly continue forever, but it's filled with massive waves, lightning storms and sharks.

Maybe there isn't another side?

For many of these entrepreneurial seafarers, they've come too far to turn around now. They couldn't possibly face the people they left behind on the shore. It would be too embarrassing, particularly those who never believed in them to start with. Choosing to turn back at this point would mean that they failed in their quest.

"You only fail if you give up," says the world around them.

As the fear of running out of fuel starts to creep in, they ease off on the engine and start to float aimlessly in whichever direction the wind and tide take them — unfulfilled, frustrated, overwhelmed and confused.

They still have that same desire inside to reach the promised land, and they just know there is this dream destination out there somewhere. They're reminded of it daily on social media and at every marketing outlet going. But they have no bloody clue where it is!

Then all of a sudden, when the chips are down, they see a little glint of light on the horizon. They hear someone's voice shouting...

"Over here! I'll show you the way!"

They think to themselves, "I've struck gold; this is the destination I've been dreaming of!"

Back on that engine goes, and they're off and running again. They have their new "guide" waxing lyrical about how amazing the other side is when they get there...

"Look at all these shiny things."

"If I can do it, you can do it."

"It's as easy as 1, 2, 3..."

But what actually happens next?

Part-way across the lake in that new direction, another glint of light flickers on the horizon in the opposite direction. But this time, it's a bigger, shinier glint and comes with a louder voice. The voice is shouting, "No, no, no, that's not where you want to go, don't trust that person. You want to go this way!"

The mind ticks, "Maybe they're right; maybe I've been too quick in my actions, maybe that is the easier, quicker route to my destination."

So a full turn to starboard, and off they go again in that new heading. Before long, they realise they're running low on fuel. All this to-ing and fro-ing and following all these so-called "experts" and "gurus" has led them to nowhere. Once again, they're lost, confused, and even more frustrated. Not to mention that they still have no idea where they're going!

Now I'm not sure about you, but this was me for periods of my life. I would have these great plans of building a business, becoming a millionaire and have endless ideas of what I wanted to do. So I would charge off full steam ahead in a certain direction, spending hours upon hours trying to make shit stick to a wall.

I'd then get distracted by someone selling a new training course, or by a seemingly easy & quick result that I wanted, so I did what everyone around me seemed to be doing and followed. I "invested in my education". I "sacked the boss".

But it didn't take long before I became overwhelmed, stressed and confused. Not to mention the thousands upon thousands of pounds I'd pissed down the drain making one bad decision after the other.

Now, I don't blame the self-professed gurus or the expert marketers who hooked me and reeled me in. Often their content has been pretty good.

I blame myself.

It was only when I took the time to seriously think about and write down *exactly* what I wanted from life that I realised over half of this "stuff" was completely irrelevant to me and was a complete distraction.

I needed to work out what I already had, and exactly where I wanted to go. Then just focus on one or two things that would actually get me there. I knew property was my answer, as it complimented my existing skill sets as well as ignited a passion inside me. I had a lot of transferable skills from my engineering background, as well as some refurb experience from knocking around a few houses in my youth.

I just needed to find one or two strategies that worked for me and once I honed in on those, the needle started to move.

I picked up my first deal in my first year, then a second in my second year. My portfolio was growing and my property venture was off and running. But then I very quickly hit my next challenge, one I now see occurring more frequently than ever before in other property investors…

I would spend a load of energy finding a "deal", then I would do loads of work doing the "deal". Once it was then finished I would then have loads of downtime in between projects whilst I had to find and secure the next "deal". I would have these major feast and famine periods and it felt like I was starting from scratch every time.

I realised I wasn't treating this venture like a proper business, I was just focusing on the here and now. The quick, immediate win. This led to massive highs and massive lows. I would have these huge cashflow issues for months at a time where I would invest all my eggs in that next deal. Deals would pass me by. Opportunities would come and go because my hands were tied. Then I would have a spike in capital when I was able to refinance or sell.

A lack of structure and lack of a solid business plan created a number of further issues like doing everything myself, paying more than I needed to for services and refurbs, and having a constant anxiety and feeling that I could be doing more than I was.

I took another step back to reflect and realised I was doing some things well, but not others. I wrote down what worked and what didn't, and decided the only way to scale this thing would be to create a framework.

This framework transformed my life, and now that you are reading this book, means that the dreams I once had of building a successful business, becoming a millionaire, and having the freedom to choose how I spend my time are now a reality.

And it is all thanks to my Do More Deals Framework™.

The essence of the framework lies in its name and is something I have been teaching for a number of years. I have not only seen it work first hand but have seen others implement it with consistent success.

There's nothing I find more fulfilling than witnessing others triumph; engage and collaborate with the sole purpose of supporting each other; and seeing them use my experiences to better their lives.

Both myself and others have been able to create multiple other businesses off the back of our property investment businesses. Businesses in their own right that add additional income streams to our personal wealth. But none of this would have happened had I not figured out this framework.

Having now implemented this framework over a number of years, seeing the results - as well as teaching it to countless students and seeing their results - has led me to want to write this book to share it with you.

This book is all about this framework. It's designed to guide you in building more clarity behind your goals and aspirations; and to help grow your confidence in finding, attracting and structuring more profitable deals for you and your business.

It's your turn to be a winner, and I'm excited to guide you on this journey.

We're In The Eye Of The Storm

I have wanted to write a book for over five years but to be perfectly honest with you, I haven't felt that the timing was quite right. Now however is the right time because I believe we are currently experiencing a very unique set of circumstances within the property sector in the UK.

We are in this perfect storm of:

1. **Increasing cost of debt** - interest rates have risen consistently and many property owners are still on very low interest fixed rate mortgages that have yet to mature. When they do peoples cashflow is going to decrease and cost of living is going to rise.
2. **Rising inflation** - leading to an increased cost of living meaning people are going to start to feel the pinch.
3. **Media induced AP fear in the economy and property market** - a rising fear will lead people to sit on their hands and effective become paralysed into taking any risks or actions.
4. **Wars and worldwide unrest** - leading to people sitting on cash in the bank, many people becoming afraid to say things through fear of might happen and further increased living costs through oil tankers being hijacked, exporters being unable to export, and the UK being one of

the largest importers of goods having to pay more per item.

5. **Changes in legislation** - within the property sector is leading to many investors exiting the market and running away.
6. **Increasing number of "gurus" and education companies** - that are regurgitating unregulated, unrefined nonsense and relying on high pressure sales and marketing tactics that leads to overwhelm, confusion and poor results.

As a result of these circumstances, a lot of people are already struggling financially, or about to struggle big time. Yet amongst the challenge, struggle and pain that many will experience, a lot of others are about to win. And they're about to win *big time.*

When there is increased uncertainty, there is always increased opportunity and I strongly believe that those who are willing to step up in this moment and take some risks are going to be the ones who will prosper. The potential upside to which could be huge.

In this book, I'm going to take you through each step of the Do More Deals Framework™ in detail but for now, let's take a look at what the framework consists of.

Psyche

At the forefront of the Do More Deals Framework™ lies the initial component: adopting a Deal Makers' Mindset™. This step is where you will be exploring your psyche's role in attaining success in the world of property and business.

Both success and failure are highly predictable and it is all linked to how one thinks.

We each have a set of ingrained blueprints for how we see the World and operate within it. Understanding those that are serving you, and those that are holding you back is the most important aspect of this framework.

Shedding any limiting beliefs and adopting more of a growth mindset are the true secrets to success so we're going to get clear on how you can embrace a mindset that fosters confidence in adapting to changes, doing more deals and achieving your goals.

Plan

As the saying goes - Piss Poor Planning equals Piss Poor Performance.

To launch any business effectively, you need to craft a comprehensive plan that consists of the potential resources you can access and leverage. This solid plan will build clarity behind your focus and actions and serve as your guide as you unlock new opportunities and grow.

We're going to be unpacking The 3M Plan™ built upon the key identifiers —Mandate, Mission, and Metrics— to build solid goals, monitor progress and move the needle right away.

Position

With a solid business plan and newfound clarity gained from the first two steps, it's time to answer the crucial question: Why Me?

We're going to go through The Deal Triangle™ — three essential elements vital for any property deal's success. This is where you'll be able to assess current resources, identify gaps, and strategically position yourself in the market to attract what you want.

Promotion

Everybody thinks this part is simple: And it is when you know what you're doing. But get this wrong from the outset and you can find yourself putting in a lot of effort with little to show for it.

We'll be sharing The Visibility Builder™ methodology exploring tailored strategies aimed at boosting your visibility, building your credibility, and getting clear on your message.

Prospect

During the good ol' days, prospectors ventured into the mountains to find gold nuggets concealed in creek beds and deep caverns. However as a 21st century property entrepreneur, your quest for ideal opportunities is a little more complex.

What works, what doesn't? The Deal Finder™ will take you through the four things that actually work, that will keep the cost to your business down, and how you can implement them today.

Persist

Everyone aspires to discover the ideal prospect, establish a meaningful connection, and quickly secure the most significant deal. However, the practical reality of Doing More Deals isn't as straightforward as getting a Yes on the first go.

In the final stage of the framework, we're going to run through The Easy AS…F Method™ where you'll learn how to streamline processes, maximise efficiency, and enhance the chances of securing deals. It really is as easy as f…

As you can tell, there's a bunch of stuff to grasp before jumping straight into that boat and pushing it out onto Lake Property Entrepreneurship.

The Do More Deals Framework™ is a step-by-step process so follow each step before jumping to the next. If you skip around thinking you've nailed the previous sections prior to reading this book, you'll miss putting the whole picture together. Trust me, it's worth going through it methodically.

Finally, I know that starting or scaling any business can be intimidating and it is never as easy as anyone says it is. I'm not here to pull the wool over your eyes but provide you with lessons, frameworks and as much support as I possibly can to ensure you achieve success in a fraction of the time I did.

When you follow the steps in the Do More Deals Framework™ and begin implementing your new found knowledge not only will you find more deals, but you'll start to see that people will start bringing you more and more opportunities. More people will want to work with you, and more people will want to entrust you with growing their money for them.

Soon enough, you'll establish a direct line of credit into the millions, build a personal income well into the six figures and all whilst building a proper investment business that has a value in its own right beyond just the individual value of the property assets themselves...

Oh and you'll have successfully assembled a team and network of incredible people around you who make the journey and adventure truly fulfilling!

To provide additional support to you I've created additional resources for you to download and work on whilst advancing through the framework throughout the book.

Visit the additional resources area at https://www.propertyentrepreneurs.club/dmd-book-resource to access these valuable materials.

PART 1
PSYCHE

CHAPTER 1

"WHY?" AND THE SUCCESS CYCLE

Let me tell you a bit about my family background. My parents are both opticians, and when we were kids, they decided to take a leap of faith and start their own business.

My dad has a fairly no-nonsense, straightforward approach to life. He's very practical and is very much about getting things done. "Don't mess around or over think it, just get on with it." I can hear him say as I write this.

My mum, whilst also practical, is on the other hand more creative and takes a more considered approach to life.

They both have vision to be fair to them, in different ways and are open to new ideas however if you cannot explain something with sound logic and science, it's always going to be a hard sell for my Dad.

Because of this upbringing, and perhaps because of being a boy and wanting to model my father, I didn't give much thought to the role of our mind in shaping our actions and behaviours. I didn't really acknowledge, nor take time to understand how our thoughts play a significant role in what we do. I just, got on with it.

Sure, we'd talk about self-confidence, be often encouraged to try things and be told "we can do it" , but in my household growing up, having a deep discussion about how we were feeling and understanding our emotions wasn't something that was particularly focused on.

But you know what? Life's got its way of teaching us the lessons we need to learn and through the experiences of going to university, getting my first job in the big wide world, buying my first property and then starting my first business... I've sure come to understand that our mindset is an absolute game-changer.

The way we think about ourselves and understand how we tick will either hold us back or propel us forward.

Deal-Maker Mindset

Here's something I wholeheartedly believe in: each and every individual, *without exception,* possesses the potential for unlimited success. Whatever that success might mean to them.

Every person on this planet is born with the exact same blank sheet of paper in terms of their knowledge. As we make what is the most dangerous and risky journey we'll ever make in our lifetimes and enter into this world - we are all the same in terms of what we know about the world.

Everything is instinctive as a one minute old baby. From that point onwards what we learn about the World and importantly *how* we learn to think is all learned behaviour.

Whilst I appreciate that not everyone starts from the same footing in terms of the environments they are born into, everyone in their own way has the capability to do and achieve whatever they want. For some it will be harder than others but it's environmental and we *can* change our environments.

But here's the thing that breaks my heart – not everyone is willing to do what it takes to try and change. Not everyone is willing to make difficult decisions and as a result so many people walk around with this nagging feeling of failure or with chips on their shoulders about how they have been dealt a bad hand.

We live in a world that is getting faster by the minute, and we are constantly being reminded by subliminal messaging, marketing, and the media of all the things we don't yet have.

That fast car, that luxury holiday, the bulging bank account, the athletic physique...

If we allow it, for which I can see millions and millions of people doing, we carry this haunting notion that we are consistently falling short of what is expected of us. These negative and limiting beliefs stop us in our tracks, make us question everything about what is possible and drag us down. It can be paralysing to the point where it becomes all we think about.

I know this because I battle with self doubt regularly. I compare myself to others above me and wonder why I don't have more than I have. However, I have come to learn that this thinking is completely normal and is dictated to us by the capitalist World we live in. The key is to learn how to manage and balance those thoughts with regular moments of appreciation and acknowledgement.

The thing is, success and failure follow certain patterns and can be predicted to some extent – they simply don't just happen out of the blue. If there's one thing certain about the road to success, it's that the primary obstacle that can hinder your progress is your own decision to either hold yourself back, or allow yourself to prosper.

Overthinking and constantly comparing yourself to others impedes your growth more than you think. The key is to break free from these mental barriers. Believe it or not, I actually don't read a lot of self-help books because I know how my head works. When I read self-help books, it often sends my mind into overdrive thinking about all the things I could or should be doing. I then end up down a rabbit hole seeking out answers to problems that didn't actually exist in my mind until I read the book.

I often read articles and publications to increase my knowledge and skill up, but take a lot with a pinch of salt otherwise I then begin to overthink things. Ironic hey, given that I've just written this very self-help book that you're reading now.

However I also recognise and understand that the way *I think,* is possibly different to the way others think. Whilst you may relate to me, others won't. So I fully appreciate that you will cast your own judgement on the effectiveness and impact of this book in your life. You might love it, you might think it's a load of dross. I'm cool with it either way but if this helps just one person to make significant changes in their life for the better then I'm happy.

The key reason for me writing this book is because I've always wanted to write a book. I've always wanted to be able to share what I've learnt, the way I think and provide value to help others achieve. So rather than overthink, question my ability or whether I'm worthy of writing such a book, I've taken my dad's advice and "just got on with it".

What's this got to do with you and with property?

Well, it is this kind of mindset that I want you to start adopting when it comes to building your business in property and seeking to structure more deals. You have to shatter any barriers, break off any shackles of self doubt, and give less of a shit about what is about to happen next. Because let's be honest, it's you giving too much of a shit about things that has prevented you from achieving the things you've wanted to date but not yet achieved. You might want to read that bit again...

Caring about what people might think about you, or what they might say about you will hold you back. I can tell you for free right now, that no one actually cares anywhere near as much as you think they do about *what* you do or don't do from now on (as long as it's within the law of course).

So it's time to set yourself free from any self doubt, any unnecessary comparisons and embrace the journey. Take some risks. Be outspoken. Aim high and pull the trigger.

The Belief And Success Cycle

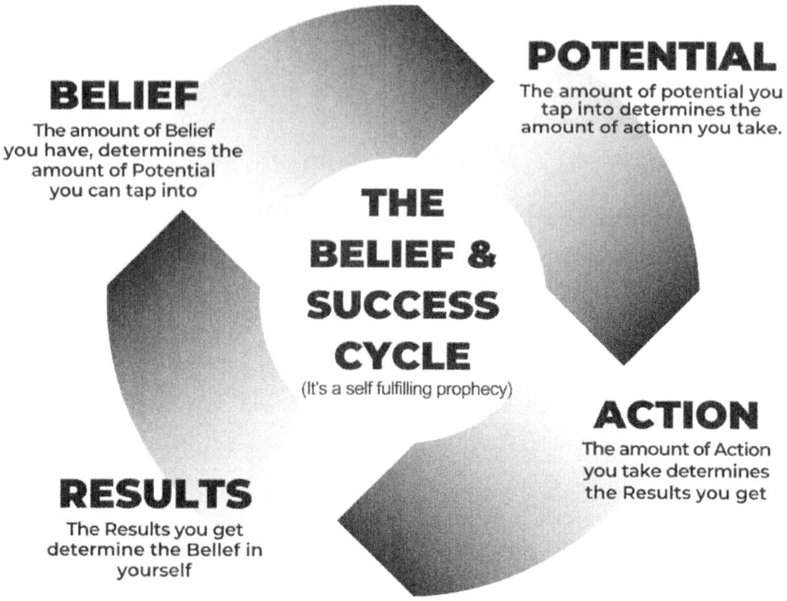

The Belief and Success Cycle isn't anything new and I certainly do not wish to take the credit for it, however it is something I agree with and it helps put into context this next section.

When it comes to building a successful business, the results that we ultimately generate all stem from our initial internal beliefs. How we think, feel, and what we BELIEVE is possible influences the level of POTENTIAL we tap into within ourselves.

This then sparks the ACTIONS we take to try and achieve the outcome, which in turn leads to a particular set of RESULTS. These results will then either reinforce, or perhaps change the initial belief that sets the cycle off.

For example, one of my earliest clients, Luke, approached me a number of years ago having listened to one of my talks about my journey and how I started out in property. He had always had a burning desire to get into property as a full time thing but after a couple of years of flipping houses he felt nowhere nearer to his goal.

His strategy up until this point was that he had been buying houses to move into. Renovating them to add some value. Selling and moving on to the next one. Each time he was moving his family into a wreck, spending countless hours outside of an already busy full time job to keep costs low and renovate each property. He would sell them, make a few quid and go again. His aim was to save enough cash using this strategy to put towards an investment property to then build a secondary income stream. Eventually getting to the point when this secondary income exceeded his primary income from his job.

Having sat with him over a brief coffee I identified that whilst he had an overall belief that property was the right vehicle for him - and so was tapping into some potential and taking some actions accordingly.

He also had a number of limiting beliefs which were actually holding him back from actually moving the needle in a bigger way.

You see, one of his biggest limiting beliefs was that he never felt experienced enough or knowledgeable enough to start working with investors and raise funding for deals. He always thought he had to do it by himself because in his words "why would anyone work with me and lend me money?"

He's a great guy and since that coffee we've worked together ever since. He's humble and he cares a lot about others and about his reputation which are all great traits to have but like everything, it needs balancing. Because if you let them, such traits can hold you back.

I told him that after working with me for a few short months, where we would focus primarily on his beliefs - he would raise enough money from investors to buy and complete a property deal without putting in any of his own money.

Within 4 months he had found a deal that required a total of £125,000 to buy, refurbish and exit (and that he didn't need to move his family into). He raised close to every single penny from three separate individuals, putting only a couple of thousand pounds of his own cash into it. Within seven months he had remortgaged everything back out, paid back his investors and had a rental property to his name.

Perhaps you may wish to write down examples in the past where you have a belief that something was possible and then achieved it? Then ask yourself to do the opposite, i.e when have you wanted something but not fully believed in certain things that have prevented you from achieving those results?

Be Careful Who You Listen To

Sometimes, just a single thought can change the complete trajectory of your success. Whether that thought comes into your head because you've just read a single article on how the property market might crash, or heard someone's opinion on the buy-to-let strategy no longer being viable.

This is why we have to be very careful and very conscious as to who we listen to and what information we absorb. Remember, we are surrounded by constant messaging that either we are not enough, don't have enough and need something else.

We also live in a capitalist world where people, companies and governments are competing for "eye-balls" and guess what attracts the most eye-balls?

FEAR!

So no wonder headlines are constantly negative, no wonder most social media posts are linked to something bad happening because that's how they hook us. But let's get real for a second - no one is a fortune teller and actually knows what's about to happen. So stop falling for it!

This is why we need to be very clear on what it is that we *want and believe* we can achieve. Then go out there and take the *actions* to reinforce our beliefs with the information that supports the *result*.

"Shoot for the moon. Even if you miss, you'll land among the stars." — Norman Vincent Peale

To be successful, it's essential to maintain a positive mindset and believe in your abilities. You must set ambitious goals for yourself, whether that is finding multiple opportunities within the next few months or reaching a specific financial milestone (net worth or portfolio value) within a few years. By setting the bar high, if you only make it part way, it's going to be a lot further along than where you are now.

To truly achieve success, in my view, it's imperative that we each cultivate a positive and empowering mindset. We need to wholeheartedly believe in our capabilities to overcome challenges and remain focused regardless of what others say. The entrepreneurial world is a fickle one but if you expect to step out on your own, be your own boss and achieve things that you aspire to achieve - you need to remember that this isn't the norm. So others around you are going to pull you back. They are not going to believe in you. But none of that matters. The only thing that matters is whether you believe in yourself. That belief in yourself is the driving force that will propel you forward.

I can certainly relate to the power of beliefs in shaping our journeys. Earlier in my life, I used to harbour doubts about my capacity to become a millionaire. I always felt that my upbringing instilled a mindset that discouraged such lofty dreams. But with time and introspection, I came to realise that my upbringing has little to do with it, it was simply a lack of belief in myself that was holding me back.

Structure, Discipline And Habits

Working for yourself also demands discipline and structure. In our younger years we grow up with well-defined routines, we go to school at 8am, maybe have tea at 5pm, then we're off to bed like clockwork. The same is true when we find a job. There's usually a defined start and finish, roles and responsibilities are set and you are expected to operate within your defined parameters.

When working for yourself, the onus is now completely on you to develop the skill of self-discipline. All those pre-set routines and structures go out the window. Allow me to share a quick personal anecdote that underscores the importance of structure, discipline and self belief.

In 2015, I took the plunge into full-time property investment. However, in the early years I encountered stumbling blocks due to a lack of discipline and self-confidence.

I found it really hard to establish a structure and focus. This lack of discipline contributed to unproductive habits, like staying in bed longer than necessary or procrastinating too often and easily. I would then make silly decisions and start chasing get rich quick schemes in the attempt to mask my lack of focus but landed a quick win.

This all culminated in a breakdown in the spring of 2017, just when my wife was pregnant with our first child. The immense responsibility of supporting my growing family weighed heavily on my shoulders. I was out walking one day with my wife, who was heavily pregnant at the time, and she could sense things were not right so asked me how I was. And I just bawled my eyes out.

It was a horrible time but it was during that period when I recognised the significance of understanding oneself and taking responsibility for the thoughts and actions that you take.

I needed to take some time to build clarity behind what I was trying to achieve, and become more purposeful and committed to my goals. Establishing a shared vision with my wife was a major help and involving her in the journey was a game changer. It was no longer just my journey, but it was ours. We created a vision and a plan, identified what I was good at, and where I needed some support.

Breaking this down with someone else and realising that you are not alone on the journey is an absolute game-changer. So if you ever feel stuck or devoid of optimism, seeking support from others or seeking professional guidance can make all the difference. Practising this self-awareness enables you to develop a mindset for success.

Fortunately I recognised some major faults relatively early in my career and life. To counteract the challenges, I created clear boundaries between work and personal life. I secured a separate office space and set specific time schedules for tasks. This instilled a sense of focus, whilst also ensuring multiple aspects were continuously progressing without feeling like something was becoming too big and overwhelming. This newfound structure empowered me to be more productive, more focus and more empowered. I rekindled *belief* in myself and *belief in what* I could achieve. Unsurprisingly from that point onwards I've rarely looked back as results started to drop, income started to rise and this only just reinforced the beliefs in my abilities.

Having structure and discipline therefore is essential for success when you work for yourself. Creating a schedule and establishing a dedicated workspace can make a difference, but you have to find out what works for yourself.

Whilst life isn't always perfect, and you will have your challenges as we all do, you can flourish with the right mindset and approach.

Fixed Mindset vs Growth Mindset

I would like you to ask yourself the following questions:

- What's driving you to want to do this?
- What excites you?
- What are you afraid of?
- What inspires you and pushes you forward?
- What is holding you back?
- Are you confident in your abilities?
- What limiting beliefs do you hold?

There are two ways to approach the way we think about specific elements in our life, either with a *fixed mindset* or a *growth mindset*.

Personally, some of the beliefs that have held me back in the past have all been down to having a fixed mindset over certain aspects. For example, I used to have a limiting belief that I can't sell to people. I hated the thought of making people feel uncomfortable or the feeling of rejection when people declined my offer. I would shy away from the task of picking up the phone to sell something, whether it be a deal I was looking to raise funding on, or a deal I was looking to sell onto an investor. And it was my fixed mindset that wouldn't allow me to overcome this belief.

It wasn't until someone highlighted to me that we are always selling - whether that is when trying to convince someone to your point of view, or to do something in a particular way - which is when I started to understand my particular limiting belief.

I also realised that I didn't like selling because I personally didn't feel comfortable in certain situations when I was being sold to - I didn't like the emotional pressure I would be put under - so I blanketed the whole act of *selling* into something I didn't like doing. However, I'm actually naturally pretty good at selling.

It wasn't until someone highlighted to me that it is often *the way* in which something is sold that is more important than the act of selling itself. Just because I don't feel comfortable when someone puts a certain amount of sales pressure on me, doesn't mean I have to do the same thing.

It was at this point that I realised it's all about how we frame things. When we understand that and understand that we can change anything with enough dedication and focus that you recognise that you can achieve anything you want.

I now feel totally comfortable in selling myself, my business, products, investments, programmes and services because I do it my way and I am totally confident that the thing I am selling will 100% benefit the other party.

My fixed mindset on selling as a whole was understandably holding me back - which further led me to my breakdown in 2017 and it has only been since I've adopted more of a growth mindset that things really started to take off.

I believe you lean towards the growth mindset, otherwise you wouldn't be reading this book. But it's crucial to question if you genuinely believe in some of the ideas and thoughts in your mind. Or whether you have just adopted them because they seem good based on what someone else has said. Do you actually believe them?

Consider your beliefs about money for example:

- Is money the root of all evil, or can it bring about good things?
- Do you need money to make money, or are ideas enough to lead to success?
- Is making money hard, or are there more opportunities available now than ever before?

Reflect on your genuine beliefs about these statements.

Many people are taught negative beliefs about money, scarcity, and the need to work excessively hard to succeed. Personally, I believe that while hard work is a good trait to have, it's not the only ingredient for success. It's the mindset within the person who is working hard that makes all the difference.

My beliefs have changed over time and in turn so have my actions. Importantly, the results (and not only in a monetary sense) are now in a completely different league to where they have been before taking the time to identify them.

Don't be afraid to challenge your own beliefs. It's so crucial to recognise and challenge any limiting beliefs if you wish to unlock your potential and go out there and do more deals. Be honest with yourself, drop any ego you might have and embrace a growth mindset.

Perhaps you could try the following:

- Write 10 great things about yourself.
- What are some limiting beliefs that you tell yourself?
- What could you take more responsibility over in your life?

Maybe make a vow to yourself today – a vow to no more holding yourself back, no more allowing any self-doubt to cloud your vision. It's time to embrace your uniqueness and take responsibility for your results.

Whilst I guarantee this journey won't be easy, because greatness is never forged without challenges, you can achieve whatever you dream of. I see your aspirations and I know that you wouldn't be reading this book, if you didn't yearn for more success.

So I want you to close your eyes for a moment and envision the future you desire. See it clearly, like a vivid painting in your mind. Now, let's make that vision a reality – one step at a time, one decision at a time.

Make today DAY ONE, and drop the ONE DAY.

PART 2
PLAN

CHAPTER 2

WHERE ARE YOU NOW

In order to turn any vision or dream into reality we need a solid Plan. But like in any journey, whether it's in property, life or business, before we can start mapping out exactly how to achieve our desired results, we have to take stock of where we are right now.

Consider it like a GPS, or Google Maps - in order to plot the quickest or most direct route, it needs to know two things:

1. Your starting point - i.e. where you are right now
2. Your destination - i.e. where you want to go

Hence, understanding where you are right now is the first crucial step. This is often overlooked and under-appreciated by the majority of early property entrepreneurs. If I had £1 for every time I have met or spoken to a property entrepreneur who is a few years into their journey but have not written out a business plan and are finding themselves going round in circles, then I probably wouldn't have as many mortgages as I do now!

While the urge to uncover all answers immediately may be strong, starting with a systematic, step-by-step approach is the key. Understanding your current position is the foundation for plotting your path and comprehending your destination ahead. Each person - despite all starting out the same at birth - has since learnt different things in their lives to date in terms of knowledge, values but also in terms of how they think. Therefore each person is unique and has their own starting point. What you can do right now is to spend time identifying where you are at this present moment.

The knowledge gained from this chapter will serve as your guide, providing a clear view of your accomplishments and how far you've come already. Drawing a line in the sand today will also enable you to monitor your progress from this point forwards. This will lead to both future empowerment in yourself and in some cases, the necessary kick up the backside we all sometimes require.

In this section we are going to be asking ourselves some important questions as follows:

- How much time are you currently able to dedicate to your property business?
- How much money do you have access to?
- How much money do you make annually?
- What's your net worth and level of assets vs liabilities?
- What level of business and property relevant expertise do you have?
- What skills do you have that are transferable?
- What values do you hold?
- What experience can you lean on?

Now let's dive into each identifier for assessing where you currently are at the moment.

Time

Everyone has the same 24 hours in a day. The key question to ask yourself is, how much of that time will you actually access and prioritise for your property business moving forward?

This question holds immense significance because often have you heard people say, "I don't have time for that," whether it's reviewing a deal, making a call, or going out to a local evening networking event.

So how high of a priority does your property business hold in your journey? Because if it is not very high, then you are unlikely to take as many actions as someone who makes it top priority.

We often find ourselves filling our time with various tasks to the extent that we might not have time for what truly matters. A question I always come back to, and you may wish to write this down on a post-it on your workspace is: What will move the needle in my business (or life) the most?

Perhaps take a look at your current schedule and list of "to-dos" – is it heavily occupied with items that won't move that needle? How are you prioritising your property business in your life?

I get it, life gets busy with work and other responsibilities, but remember why you're doing this in the first place. You want to create a better life, financial security, more choice, flexibility and build a legacy (or whatever your motivators are). When you face tough decisions or distractions, always come back to your "why." Let that drive you to find the time you need.

Grab a pen and paper and jot down how much time you can currently devote to your property venture each week. Make yourself accountable and stick to that time commitment. If you think you can invest 10 hours a week, go for it. It's actually incredible what you can achieve in 10 hours with clarity over which actions move the needle and true focus.

If you feel you can't find that much time, that's cool, but just come back to see how your future will look like. Perhaps take a close look at your schedule and see where you can create more time for your new life. Remember, this is about building your future, creating extra income, uncovering new opportunities and experiences. You are in control. You can either make excuses and never get there, or take ownership and make it happen.

Money

There are two elements to this bit.

1. **What money do you currently have and make**

Knowing your net worth is a crucial metric to know, as it tells you not just how much money and wealth you currently possess, but also what potential resources you can access and leverage. Most people are aware of their income, but not as many are familiar with their monthly or yearly expenses. Understanding where your money is going is just as important as knowing where it's coming from because it directly affects your timeline to success.

It's important to have a well-structured budget that itemises all your expenses. Having a yearly budget is recommended, especially in a property business, where income may not come in consistently on a monthly basis. This way, you can plan your cashflow effectively and have a buffer to cover your living expenses for the entire year. Being financially prepared and having a buffer gives you the freedom to take risks in your business and aim for bigger achievements.

Assessing your current financial situation starts with understanding your net worth.

Assets - Liabilities = Your Net Worth

Knowing your net worth helps you track your progress, set goals, and measure your financial success over time. To calculate your net worth, list the values of all your assets including cash, properties, investments, pensions, insurance policies and personal valuables. E.g. anything that you could sell off to raise capital if you had to.

Then, list your liabilities, including loans, debts, mortgages, credit card balances and taxes owed. Subtract your liabilities from your assets to get your net worth.

As part of the Property Entrepreneurs Club we provide all our members with templates for calculating their net worth but also managing their personal finances as this skill is fundamental for building solid foundations to financial success.

Regularly reviewing and tracking your net worth empowers you to make informed financial decisions and work towards your goals. It's a crucial step in strategic planning and managing your finances effectively.

2. What money could you access?

In the property world, it's crucial not to underestimate the amount of money that is available. Money is everywhere.

Whether it's from friends and family, banks or private investors - money is everywhere. Most of the time we think that we have very little access to money but if there was an emergency and you needed money, we would find it, it's a matter of knowing where to look and having something compelling enough to convince others to want to give it to you.

Having been in the property game for a while, I get the sense that there is some sort of taboo or shame in approaching family members or close friends for money. There is this sense that we should all be going out there to meet that Arabian Billionaire Sheik or that high flying banking CEO who works at the top of Canary Wharf who is going to become our saviour "angel investor".

Now not to say this can't happen, and one day it will but it all depends on your starting point. For most it is understanding where you are and recognising that the biggest hurdle most people have when trying to "find money" is trust.

Let's be honest, if a complete stranger walked up to you on the street and asked you to invest £100,000 with them on a property deal they've just found, regardless of how much experience and knowledge they have you would take some convincing to say yes. There is simply no trust there.

So why do so many people in property think that they can just buy a complete stranger a coffee and they will be willing to invest in them? The number of property "gurus" and training companies I see out there telling people to just "book in those coffees" baffles me.

For a number of people, there is money just sitting there in the bank waiting for you to access with people who already like and trust you - whether this is your friends, work colleagues or family.

Now I appreciate this is not going to apply to everyone, which is why we are doing this exercise because everyone's starting point is different. But for many, your parents, grandparents, uncles, long-lost second aunts once removed who you're friends with on Facebook but haven't seen since you were 8 years old could be sitting there with bulging bank accounts that you never knew about and could be the bank you're looking for. The main question is, have you ever asked them?

For many, again not all, these people would only be too happy to invest in you and support your future. I certainly would prefer to help a relative or friend than some complete stranger I met at a networking event once. Wouldn't you want to help make your family or friends wealthier rather than anyone else?

Perhaps write a list of at least five people or places you could go to access money within the next five days. Remember Luke who I mentioned earlier? He thought he didn't know anyone with cash. Turns out one of his investors was his mum who had £50k saved in the bank waiting for the day he asked her to invest in him!

Knowledge

"You don't know what you don't know, but you do know what you do know."

Many times, we underestimate our own knowledge because we think we don't know enough. However, it's essential to acknowledge what we do know. I could bet you £50 that if I stuck you in front of someone who has zero knowledge about property investing you could speak fluently and confidently about property investing for at least 10 minutes.

Recognising what you do know is important when it comes to reinforcing self belief, but also when speaking with others and structuring deals. As we will cover later, knowledge, confidence and experience are key elements to pulling deals together.

Equally as important at this stage is to begin identifying gaps in your knowledge. Have you considered the areas in which you need to brush up on?

- Do you know how to analyse prospective deals?
- Do you know what a deal is yet?
- Do you know what strategies are available to you?

When faced with gaps in knowledge, ask yourself who can help you. Who can you learn from, and what training will help you to bridge those gaps?

Don't just jump onto the next available training course that captures your attention on social media. Take a calculated approach because when you do this, you begin to ask better questions and start seeing quicker results.

If you do not yet know what your strategy is, or if you lack clarity, own this fact. Be honest and seek the relevant guidance. Don't just plug the hole with more information that may not be relevant to you.

Seeking guidance and learning from others is a valuable way to grow and fill in any missing pieces of knowledge. Do not be afraid to let the guard down and seek these people out. Building relationships with others with more knowledge and experience will not only give you access to answers when you need them but will also give you a safety blanket for when you are asked a direct question but do not know how to answer. That's when you can use your get out of jail free card...

"That's a great question, and I know the exact person who can answer this. Leave it with me and I'll come back to you."

Values

Your values are a large part of your personal identity and shape your decisions and actions. Taking some time to identify them will also help you make better decisions, employ better staff and work on projects that are in harmony with your personal beliefs.

In property, and in business, we are constantly required to make multiple decisions on a daily basis. When faced with various opportunities or challenges, you can assess them based on whether they align with your values or not. This helps you stay true to your principles, true to your plan and avoid making decisions that might compromise your integrity or long-term vision.

I have been introduced to so many different opportunities over the years and naturally as an entrepreneur you do consider them. However I have spent - or rather wasted - several hours and days considering deals that just simply did not align with my values. And yet, it took me too long to arrive at the decision to walk away. Whether that was working with someone who just didn't feel right, or a scheme that sailed too close to the wind on certain issues. Nowadays I am able to spot opportunities a lot quicker but just as importantly, turn down opportunities much quicker as this enables me to move forward without getting bogged down into abortive work. Much of this has been to spend time on identifying and understanding my values.

So time to spend some time on yours. Consider what principles are most important to you, what motivates you, and what you want to achieve with your property business beyond just the financial gains. Write down your values and use them as a guiding framework as you make decisions, set goals, and build your business. Be aware that it is your values that allow you to create a business that is not only profitable but also meaningful and fulfilling on a personal level.

Network

Your current network comprises people who possess what you need. They can assist you in finding what you want, be it deals, expertise, experiences, money or knowledge. Take a look at your phonebook; you might already have valuable connections right in front of you. The key is to know what it is you need and ask the right questions to tap into the resources already available to you.

It is important to have the confidence to ask for what you want without fear or what people may think of you if you did. I have found in my time that people are on the whole, much more receptive and supportive if asked a direct question. Especially when that question is related to supporting me on my journey.

By tapping into your network effectively, you can accelerate your growth, create more opportunities for yourself, and find the required support. Don't be a Lone Ranger!

Perhaps map out who you already know and make a list of your top 10 valuable connections within your property business.

- Who are they and why are they valuable to you?
- What can they support you with specifically?
- How can you improve that relationship?
- What more could you get out of the relationship?
- How could you support them and bring value to them?

Skills & Experience

Let's take a moment to recognize the skills you already have. This is really important because knowing what you are able to do will help you leverage the things you are good at and plug the gaps where necessary. It will help you make smarter decisions especially when it comes to choosing strategies, deciding what tasks to do and what to spend time learning.

What I have learnt over the years is that I do not need to know or be able to do everything. In fact being able to do everything, is the opposite of what I actually want to create for myself. I want to create a lifestyle where I don't have to do *anything* (or most realistically do very little). So why spend energy trying to learn every little detail and spend hours, days and often years perfecting how to do things?

It took me years to realise that I could move the needle much more by leveraging others and outsourcing or delegating tasks. However this wasn't always a skill I possessed. So when I realised this, I worked on improving that skill.

It also made me realise that in order to delegate more and leverage others, my goal had to be bigger to absorb the costs of outsourcing all the necessary tasks and bringing the necessary skills on board. This is when my mindset switched from being that small-time "landlord" who tried to do everything, taking precious time away from the things that truly moved the needle (doing more deals) - to one of an entrepreneur with a larger vision and a focus on building serious leveraged wealth.

So I would like you to make two lists. First, write down all the skills you're good at. What are you naturally great at? Are you a numbers whiz, a people person, or a super-efficient worker?

Then, jot down the skills you feel you need to improve. Is procrastination holding you back? Do you want to get better at managing your finances or building strong connections with others?

Skills I am Good At	Skills I need to Improve

These are the areas where you'll need to make a decision as to whether to focus on developing them yourself or outsourcing them to others. You could actually add a third column to the right of these and note whether you'll "develop" or "outsource" the skill.

Why do this? Well, it's all about prioritising and finding the right support. Recognising your strengths will help you focus on what you're already awesome at, meaning that you want to focus what you do on these. On the other hand, by identifying areas for improvement, you can work on developing these skills as you go.

As you progress, you'll start wondering: "Who can I bring in to complement my skills or help me with the things I'm not so good at?" That's the next step. You'll look at building a team to fill any skill gaps you might have. The key is to play to your strengths and build a team to leverage and scale.

It's also important to recognise any experience gained outside the property industry can be just as valuable as direct real estate experience. Every aspect of your past experiences contributes to your skill set and personal growth, making you a more well-rounded and capable property entrepreneur.

Suppose you have experience in financial management, such as budgeting, forecasting, or handling investments. You can apply those skills and experiences to assess property deals, analyse potential returns, and manage your property portfolio effectively. Could you leverage these skills and offer them to others as an additional income stream or as part of a joint venture? Life experiences also teach us so much, so which life experiences can you lean on to showcase your adaptability?

Knowing where you currently stand in terms of your existing skills and experiences allows you to capitalise on your strengths and identify areas for improvement. When we move through the Chapters in this book, it will become clearer as to when, where and how you can lean on these skills and experience to attract more opportunities into your business.

CHAPTER 3

THE THREE "Ms"

The Three M's are crucial for planning your path forward. You need to have a clear understanding of these three elements for a well-defined vision, strategy, and direction.

I alluded to this earlier - I have spoken with, coached and advised hundreds of people over the years and one of the most common challenges I see is an initial lack of clarity behind what they are actually trying to achieve. The number of property entrepreneurs I speak to who are a few years into their journey yet still don't have a solid business plan actually scares me.

I see so many common threads, one of which is that they simply lack clarity and they are going round and round in circles, trying every silver bullet that they can find. They know they want more of what I've already said.

More money. More time. More freedom. More flexibility. More choice. And there is nothing wrong with that.

But when drilled that's as far as it goes. What I see happening too often is that in the process of seeking 'more', people are actually ending up with less. Less money, less time, less freedom, less happiness. They are somewhere down that rabbit hole, bashing their head against a brick wall because nothing seems to be working.

So these next few chapters are going to cover the three most important things to mapping out a proper plan. I call them the Three M's. Because when we build out a proper, solid plan, around these Three M's we establish three things:

1. Clarity
2. Confidence (and these two things in turn produce)
3. Consistent results

What Are The Three Ms?

M #1 - The first M is your MANDATE.

Your *Mandate* effectively serves as the blueprint for how your property business operates and generates income. It is made up of two essential factors which are area and strategy.

M #2 - The Second "M" is your MISSION.

Your Mission is about understanding why you're in property, what you aim to achieve, and what your long-term goals are.

M #3 - The Third "M" is your METRICS.

Your Metrics are all about defining "what a deal is" for your business and help you to measure your progress. Many businesses refer to these metrics as KPI's (Key Performance Indicators). Without proper metrics, you will struggle to firstly identify what a deal looks like in your business, but equally whether you're actually achieving your mission and following your mandate effectively.

Our Mandate is our "how,"
Our Mission is the "why"
And the Metrics are the "what"

The 3 M's are not standalone concepts. Once you align them all together, you'll have a clear measurable roadmap for your property business journey. In this chapter, we will dive into the first of these "M's" which is our Mandate.

M#1 - Mandate

The mandate is effectively the overarching blueprint for how your business operates and makes money. It is in other words your business plan. It includes crucial components such as the specific locations you'll operate in and what has become to be known in the property industry as the "strategies" you'll use to achieve your goals.

By having a well-defined mandate, you establish the framework for your business operations, ensuring you have absolute clarity behind what you're doing. As you construct your mandate, keep these SIX vital questions in mind:

1. Who?
2. What?
3. Where?
4. When?
5. Why?
6. How?

These are always the most powerful questions to ask yourself constantly.

1. **Why?** This is always the best question to start with. Why do this? Why even bother to start this business in the first place?
2. **What?** What are you trying to achieve with this business? What are the goals? Define them with metrics. What will your exit be?
3. **When?** When do you expect to open for business and when do you expect to reach your goals? When will your exit be?
4. **Where?** Where does your business operate? Does it need a fixed office or not? Where do you intend to do "deals"? Where do you need to go or be to make these deals happen?
5. **Who?** Whom do you need to access for your business? Do you know who the first person you're going to hire is and what will their role be? Who do you need to be surrounded by?
6. **How?** How does your business actually make money? How are you going to build this into a business rather than just it being a hobby? How are you going to exit from the business?

When I started in property back in 2010 I had an immediate goal to simply get out of my job. I was working a 9-to-5 job as a civil engineer in Central

London in a large consultancy firm. I didn't see myself as an engineer long term, I wasn't really passionate about it and I didn't like the politics of the corporate world. I didn't have the flexibility or the freedom to do with my time as I wanted. My friends were often playing golf during the week, and I wanted to be able to join them when I wanted. I would see people going on these large holidays whenever they wanted but I was limited to the amount of days I could have off. You know the very usual stuff.

My initial goal when getting into property was to simply replace my income. For me at the time as a young recently graduated engineer I was on a decent salary earning £35,000 a year. Now whilst that may be a decent salary for some, in order to reach my goals I wanted to be in excess of six figures and I was never going to achieve that as an engineer so I had to do something different.

When I got into property my first goal was to simply make 35,000 pounds a year net income. Then it was to push on to the £100k mark. Because that first goal was definable and measurable, I went through the process of writing my mandate. I asked myself those six questions: Who? What? When? Where? Why? How?

I decided in order to achieve my £35k per year net income goal, I would create a small portfolio of HMO (House of Multiple Occupancy) properties. These as a strategy cash flowed well and I knew that I was able to make around one thousand pounds a month from each property (i.e. £12,000 a year). That meant I only needed three of those properties in order to hit my goal. My mandate was starting to come together.

I knew I wanted three properties of a certain size and criteria, and I set my target timeframe as three years - one per year. However I needed to do some research into *where* I could find these properties. Looking at the resources I had at the time, I had about £25,000 in savings. Buying a property with only £25k is pretty hard so it proved difficult to identify areas as the only areas within the budget were in the north of the UK. Yet I didn't want to go that far away. I wanted to operate closer to home so I could be more "hands on" (a decision I look back and regret a little bit now).

I settled on Portsmouth as my area, as it was within an hour of where I lived in Wimbledon at the time, and I already knew a little bit about the area having grown up on the Isle of Wight. Also from my research I knew I could find properties in certain areas that I could secure for around the £150,000 to £200,000 range. These were big enough to convert into large enough HMOs that would generate me at least the £1,000 per month net cashflow I required.

However, it meant that I would need to borrow some extra funds from somewhere as to buy the property with a 25% deposit, cover all the fees and then the refurb on top I was looking at at least the £75k mark. But that was all OK because with a solid business plan, I knew I would be able to raise that funding when I needed it. More on this in Chapter 7.

So now I had some answers to my questions:

1. **Why**
   a. *(Why) Am I doing this?* I wanted to quit my job as a civil engineer.
   b. *(Why) Now?* Because the sooner I start the sooner I get closer to my goal.

2. **What**
   a. *Am I trying to achieve?* To replace my income of £35,000 with property income.
   b. *Are the metrics?* To buy three properties within a price range of up to £200,000 that will generate a minimum cashflow of £1,000 per month.

3. **When?**
   a. *Will I start?* Now.

b. *Will I achieve my goal?* Within three years buying at a rate of one property per year.

4. **Where?**
   a. *Will I operate?* Portsmouth and the surrounding areas
   b. *Where will I base myself?* Remotely.

5. **Who?**
   a. *Do I need to build relationships with?* Investors - I needed to raise some equity and refurb finance from an investor. I needed to engage a mortgage broker for the initial purchases. I needed a solicitor. I needed to connect with some estate agents. I needed a letting agent.
   b. *Will I hire first and when?* When I had my three units I would employ a PA to deal with the administrative side so I could focus on doing more deals.

6. **How?**
   a. *Does my business make money?* My business effectively takes the form of an investment company, making money from holding assets which generate rental income.
   b. *Am I going to exit?* I will build a portfolio that I intend to retain long term such that this will become my future pension and legacy that I can

hand down to my children. Thus I don't plan an exit until death at which point I will need to ensure strategies are in place to hand down my portfolio tax efficiently.

By having a clear mandate in these early years, I avoided getting overwhelmed by various strategies and stayed focused on my chosen niche. It helped me stay focused on what I needed to do, and what was going to move the needle the most.

Since that first mandate I wrote out on a piece of engineers drafting paper, things have changed a bit. I have started and invested into multiple businesses, each with their own different markets and missions. My investment business has evolved and the mandate it operates by today is very different to the one I started with.

Upon reflection, my initial mandate was too small and I wasn't thinking big enough. Once I achieved my goal after those first three purchases, I lost focus and drifted for a few years. I was the guy in the boat on the lake!

I overlooked the impact that this mandate had had on my focus, actions and success in those early years. However, the learnings over the years have been that you can have multiple businesses and ventures, but having a well-defined mandate for each will keep you from going in circles and ensure you're making informed decisions along the way.

How To Pick A Strategy

For those of you reading this and still unsure as to which "strategy" to choose, I'm going to dive into a few things here that may help. But remember, although we are in property, it doesn't mean we have to follow that traditional "investor" route. You may wish to start a serviced based business that serves the multi-billion pound property sector.

For those looking to use real estate properties as the vehicles for creating wealth, there are a few key principles to recognise. Firstly, there are three stages to property.

1. There is the **Entry**. This is basically how are you going to gain control of the property.
2. There is the **Value Add** stage - this is where you create some uplift in value.
3. There is the **Exit**. Basically how you are going to generate income from the asset.

When people talk about "strategies" they are usually talking about the "exits", but sometimes these can cover the other two stages. For example, a very popular strategy currently is "Serviced Accommodation". What this means is to effectively rent properties out on a nightly basis - think Airbnb. This can be a good way to increase the income from the assets, but like everything, there are "pros" and "cons".

One "con" being the amount of management and administration that goes into running a successful portfolio of multiple units. Something many people seem to overlook when they jump into it head first without much consideration.

The other thing to realise when it comes to choosing strategies is that different strategies work best in different areas. For example, the single let rental market in London differs significantly from that in the north in areas like Middlesbrough or Liverpool.

The capital appreciation is different, but so are the yields. It's essential therefore to consider factors like capital values, rental yields, and development costs specific to each area.

Choosing the right area for your strategy is crucial. For instance, the South East may be better for choosing buy to sell type strategies - where the majority of the value is created through some form of build or development - and the exit is to sell rather than rent, due to the higher end value property prices, leading to increased potential for profit. On the other hand, areas with lower property prices and higher rental yields, like the North, may be more suitable for long term "hold" exits.

Remember, it's essential to align your strategy with the area that offers the best financial opportunities, even if it means considering locations further away.

The key obstacle to seizing opportunities and achieving higher returns is often emotional decision-making. It's natural to desire proximity to your properties for easier maintenance and management.

However, being open to exploring different locations based on financial considerations can lead to greater success.

The decision on where to operate or establish your business should be first driven by the numbers and then your personal preferences.

Ultimately finding the perfect balance is the key, but only you will be able to know what this looks like.

One of my clients, Richard, has been implementing the Serviced Accommodation strategy very successfully for the past few years. However, before working with me his strategy was quite different.

When Richard and I met, he had already built a semi-successful portfolio of mixed commercial and residential units in the Midlands. I say "semi-successful" because what he had done was working to the tune of earning him around £50,000 a year but after working together for a few years we turned that into an income in excess of £200,000 a year.

The thing I have always loved about Richard is his mindset and his desire to build something big. However, we recognised fairly early on that he was perhaps focusing on areas of his business that weren't necessarily moving the needle in a big way.

He had built a decent portfolio using all his own money, but had in effect run out of money to continue its growth and was being very busy "sustaining". His growth had stifled which led him to reaching out to me. The first question I asked him was about his mandate. Did he have one? Answer… in short, no.

So we set about working together to pull everything he already had into a single location. I.e. Where was he already? What did he already have?

We built a spreadsheet that mapped everything out from his Assets & Liabilities and his personal cashflows to his existing property portfolio with all the mortgages, rentals, personal loans - the works. This created the baseline and also uncovered a few opportunities. He had already built a small portfolio and was busy running a commercial refurbishment business where he was doing commercial fit outs and earning project management fees. He was very busy running those projects but they weren't really big enough or frequent enough to really be making big moves.

He had jumped onto some training courses about the service accommodation strategy and knew some of the theory about how it worked. So using his existing resources, his portfolio, contacts, knowledge etc., we set about writing a new mandate that would leverage these and take his business to another level. He needed to think bigger and focus on bigger wins.

Off the back of this work, we also realised that there was a big opportunity to create a separate Serviced Accommodation specialist managing company that targeted his local area as there was a gap in the market.

The opportunity was that most Serviced Accommodation "investors" have less than five units which isn't big enough to systemise, but big enough to create a time burden on those self-managing "investors".

This agency would then be set up to not only operate his own stock (thus taking from one pocket and putting it in another), but also generating a sustainable income of its own through managing other people's properties.

Hudson Property Group was born with a very clear mandate and has since been going from strength to strength.

Richard's personal income has grown, his portfolio has grown and his access to new opportunities has also grown.

The long term vision is to expand beyond his local area and he has since began franchising the Hudson brand across the country.

In the next two chapters, we will take a deep dive into understanding your mission and exploring your metrics. By doing so, you'll gain valuable insights that will help you effectively shape and complete your Mandate.

CHAPTER 4
MISSION

I assume you will have heard of "shiny object syndrome"? It's that awesome feeling when something new and exciting comes your way, and suddenly, you can't resist its pull. But actually, it just distracts you from your path and goals.

If you want to succeed in any business, not only do you need to know what your Mission is, but you've got to commit to it. It is one of the most important bricks in your foundation. If you don't have a clear understanding of where you want to go in life and why you want to go there, it's easy to get sidetracked and delay the outcomes you truly desire.

The life and business we ultimately create for ourselves is effectively the sum of all the decisions we make on a regular basis. Usually making bad decisions, or even avoiding making decisions can lead to bad outcomes.

So taking a moment upfront to establish a Mission is crucial. It helps guide your decisions and actions, and will keep you motivated. It is also there to fall back on as a reminder for when things inevitably get tough.

Your Mission is made up of three things:

1. Vision & Values

Forget about money, time or anything else that's holding you back and ask yourself these questions and write down your answers.

- Where do you see yourself in the future, maybe in 5, 10, or 15 years?
- What do you want to achieve?
- What experiences do you want to have?

Just imagine you have all the time and money in the world. The answers also don't really have to be related to property at this stage. Property is just a vehicle that will help you get there. You might have more than one dream, and that's perfectly fine. Write them all down, and then take some time to think about and prioritise them.

I use post-it notes and write down as many goals, aspirations and dreams on them. One on each note. I then stick them all over the wall in the office and over the course of a few days and weeks move them around to prioritise them. The highest priority at the top and so on. This helps you to find your ultimate destination, your main goal or set of goals.

Identifying your ultimate set of goals is super important because it will be like your driving force from now on. Whenever you have to make a decision or deal with a situation, just come back to this ultimate goal. It will guide your choices and keep you on track, moving towards what truly matters to you. There are some things you might not have thought about yet, but they could become important in the next 5, 10, or even 15-20 years.

Let me share some of my big dreams with you and how they have changed over time...

I really want to support my kids' education. Even though my daughters are still young, I'm already making plans and saving up for their college or university fund, depending on what they decide to pursue. It's something I deeply care about, and I'm factoring it into my current financial plan.

Another thing on my mind is family holidays. Over the next decade, I'm excitedly thinking about all the places we want to explore together as a family and all the experiences we want to have together. But of course, I need to consider how much these trips might cost and budget accordingly.

As I look even further ahead, like 15 or 20 years down the road, I'm starting to think about taking care of my parents as they grow older. I'd also love to show my appreciation by getting a shiny new car for my dad for all the support he's given me over the years. These are all heartfelt gestures but I also understand that it comes with financial consequences.

The key is to merge these passions with your intent on starting a property business. Ask yourself, what do you enjoy doing? If property aligns with your passions, then that's a great fit for you. However, if through reading my book, you realise that property doesn't align with your passions, that's alright too. It's a significant realisation and decision, and it allows you to move forward with clarity.

The things we are actually discussing in this book are highly transferable into other sectors. I've had clients who, after working with me for a little time, discovered that property wasn't their true passion. Instead, they found fulfilment in other areas, like starting an online business and pursuing different interests. That's perfectly fine - I'm not here to convince you to stay in property - I just want to see you get results.

The key is to identify what truly excites you and brings you joy. This clarity in your mind helps you make the right choices and create a fulfilling life and career path. This is where identifying your values from the earlier chapter as an individual is key and carries through to this step. Fundamentally, you are the heartbeat to your business, especially in the early stages as you are building it for your own personal reasons.

- Do you know who you are as an individual?
- Do you know what guides your decisions from a values perspective?

Within the Property Entrepreneurs Club we have Seven Values, all of which are built upon my personal values and the type of people I want to work with.

1. We are inclusive and respect people
2. We give more to get more
3. We are driven by results
4. We do what we say we'll do
5. We are open, real and approachable

6. We practice self awareness and humility
7. We are logical

These values help us to make decisions as a business, and I want to empower my staff to make decisions for themselves but within the guidelines of how the Property Entrepreneurs Club brand is to be perceived. Therefore all staff when faced with making decisions must ensure the outcome of those decisions fit within these values. These values also help identify with our clients and attract the type of people we want to work with within the Club.

Equally, when you start to operate in areas or with people who do not align with your personal values this starts to create friction and naturally you start to pull back from those environments. Therefore to minimise these occasions, understanding your values upfront and writing them out as part of your mission statements acts as a further guide going forward.

2. Purpose

Your purpose in building your property business is a powerful combination of two essential aspects:

1. What you do
2. What the world needs

Your purpose therefore becomes about aligning your skills, expertise, passion and means of making money, with the needs and demands of the world around you. It's about finding the sweet spot where your capabilities meet the market's requirements, creating a win-win scenario for both you, who you aim to serve, and any stakeholders.

Your purpose is essentially a safety net you can rely on during moments of uncertainty, especially when challenges arise. It acts as a constant reminder of the commitment you made to your business and provides a strong foundation to rely on when you need reassurance and guidance.

For example, in the Property Entrepreneurs Club, our purpose is:

"We help people to do more deals"

It's simple, but combines what we do, with what the world needs.

As a property developer let's say, your purpose may be something along the lines of…

"We create homes"

If you plan to focus on a more niched area of the market you may wish to tweak this accordingly. For example if you're focusing on the supported living market you may wish to use:

"We create modern, spacious homes for those with assisted living needs"

It keeps you focused and builds on that clarity that we've already covered in Chapter 3. Have a go at writing out a purpose statement and see what you come up with.

3. Goals

Goals are crucial in any business. They are not the same as the "Metrics" - we will be covering Metrics in the next Chapter as these are a bi-productive of your goals.

Goals can be tough to set, and I regularly see many people skirt around this exercise because they feel as though they are making too much of a defined commitment. Those with entrepreneurial brains will agree that we don't tend to like structure and prefer a more free and flexible approach. However as already covered in depth, *clarity is key* and so taking a moment to push yourself and set some defined goals will massively aid your chances to success.

I would suspect you would've already heard about "SMART" goals which are - Specific, Measurable, Achievable, Relevant, and Time-Bound. There's no need to reinvent the wheel here but the key is to actually set some!

Like I said, this exercise isn't particularly easy. It may take some time for you to reflect, write things down, and give it some thought. You might even need to sleep on it and come back to it later but do it otherwise you'll be out on that lake floating in the not too distant future.

Each business is different and will therefore have different goals but to give you an idea, within the Property Entrepreneurs Club our goals are linked to the size of our community, the number of paid clients, the number of tickets we sell to events and of course the revenue we generate.

As a property development company (if that's your chosen business model) you may want to set some goals around the following items:

- Number of direct letters you send per quarter/year
- Number of offers made
- Number of completed deals

- Size of your pipeline
- Gross income
- Net income
- Portfolio LTV (if you plan to hold stock)

So perhaps take a moment now to consider some of the goals you want to accomplish within the following timeframes:

- In 12 months
- In 24 months
- In 4 years
- In 6 years
- In 8 years
- In a decade

Remember, shoot for the stars and you might just land on the moon!

Rate Your Goals

Now I would like you to rate each of the goals you have just set on a scale of one to ten based on how *committed* you are to achieving them.

Commitment is more important than anything else here. So if you're not giving a goal a solid ten out of ten in terms of commitment, it's highly likely you won't achieve it. You need to be fully committed to making those goals happen. In a study on goal setting with 267 participants, Dr. Gail Matthews, a psychology professor at Dominican University in California, determined that the mere act of putting your goals into writing enhances the likelihood of achieving them by 42 percent.

Success and failure are both very predictable and much of this comes down to this exercise and your commitment. If you find that you're not fully committed to some goals, don't worry - just rewrite them, revisit them, and adjust them until they truly resonate with your wholehearted commitment. Once you have goals you are genuinely 110% committed to, then you're ready to go.

Writing your Mission Statement

Now, armed with the insights from this chapter, you should have all the tools to establish a solid mission and sense of direction. You have identified a clear destination and have a strong understanding of the underlying "why" behind it all.

To help further here are a few examples - but whatever you do, don't just copy them for ease, the more you tailor these to you, the higher chances of success you have.

Under the Property Entrepreneurs Club our mission statement is as follows - as you will see it combines our Vision, Values, Purpose and Goals all into one:

"To build a community of high-calibre people who support each other to prosper in property and to share our knowledge, educate and help 50 high-level clients complete on 50 profitable deals by the end of 2026"

By the way, at the time of releasing this book in 2024 we are well on track to achieving this but it helps keep all those involved focused.

As a Property Investment Company your mission may be something along the lines of:

"By year XXX, build a property portfolio with a gross value of £10m, producing a £300k net income per year and with a maximum debt ratio of 60%..."

Once you have all these elements, I highly recommend you print them out and put them up in your office - or wherever you work from. I also suggest every member of staff you engage with going forward - whether they are in-house or outsourced - receives a copy of these statements and buys into them.

CHAPTER 5
METRICS

Minimise the downside, and maximise the upside.

Now you know what you want to achieve and why you want to achieve it, we're going to look at building some measurable and trackable frameworks.

Our *Metrics* help us to define what qualifies as a "deal" to our business. They help us break things down effectively into manageable chunks to make it more understandable and aid for quicker decision making. For a lot of people, metrics can be quite an overwhelming element of the process. However, it is actually the most fundamental part because without it, it's difficult to assess if the deal is feasible or not.

By understanding your metrics, you can be clear on what would make a good deal and ensure that the income you expect to generate from each particular deal meets your satisfaction. Naturally, you'll want to know how much profit you can make per deal; however, if you fail to analyse your deals effectively, you might end up proceeding on a property without realising until much later that it's actually costing you more money than you're earning from it.

Ever heard the term "buying a lemon"?

I remember meeting with a lovely lady a number of years back at a training academy (which I won't name) that I did a bit of coaching and mentoring for. We'll give her the name Susan (her name wasn't Susan but you'll see why I've changed her name…)

Anyway, Susan was a genuinely lovely lady with a great heart and she signed up for this programme to the tune of several thousands of pounds, because she knew she needed some support. When chatting with her upon our first meeting, I knew instantly things weren't as Susan was making them out to be. She would skirt around my questions and as it would turn out, I could understand why. She was saving face.

Susan pulled me aside after a few months of knowing each other and came clean. She had bought a number of Rent to Rent units in the North East of England off another operator who had sold them to her for what she said to me *felt* like a "good deal" at the time. She had ten units for which she was paying three separate Landlords monthly rent, and was subletting the properties as 4-5 bed HMOs.

As part of the deal, Susan would cover all costs for running the properties such as utilities, bill, taxes etc., along with *any* contributions to maintenance. Susan also didn't live in the North East so employed a local management agent to manage the day to day which also obviously came at a cost. You could probably guess where this is heading…

Long story short, Susan had been operating this portfolio of "assets" (her term) for a couple of years and at the time of speaking was well over £100,000 in the red. She had (somehow) managed to borrow some money from another investor to put towards the venture to keep herself afloat but obviously this was just adding to her debt. Understandably, Susan was not in the best of mindsets and was incredibly stressed.

She had effectively bought a lemon and took on this portfolio without understanding any of the finances. She was incredibly naive and in her words "went on trust" of the person who sold her the portfolio.

Unfortunately Susan's case is not a rare one. I have met many other people who have jumped into deals that simply do not make any money. In every case it all stems from a lack of understanding as to how the finances work in both property and in business.

When asked if Susan had any financial information for each of the properties, I was met with a blank expression. When I mentioned the term "Profit & Loss", it was as if I was speaking another language.

Anyway, I worked with her a little bit offline (because I wanted to help) and we managed to pull together a rough profit and loss for the entire portfolio based on the headline figures she had access to. The bottom line… she was losing approximately £6,000 a month each and every month. Plus she had an outstanding debt to her investor with no way of being able to pay it back.

Now I don't share this story to put Susan down in any way. It was what it was. But I share it to warn you against the realities of jumping into deals without due care, due diligence and understanding of the finances.

Simply put, the most important aspect to any business, and in particular a property business, is understanding the financial set up to deals and structuring deals in such a way that minimise the downside, but maximise the upside.

The worst case scenario that I am willing to accept when doing deals is that I break even financially. The great Warren Buffett, arguably one of the most popular investors of all time said the following:

"Rule No 1: never lose money. Rule No 2: never forget rule No 1. Investment must be rational; if you can't understand it, don't do it. It's only when the tide goes out that you learn who's been swimming naked."

There are a number of financial engineering techniques that we take people through when they join the Property Entrepreneurs Club to achieve an unbalanced risk to reward ratio - in your favour - when structuring deals.

What Is A Deal?

Over the course of the next few pages I'm going to try and break down for you what a deal looks like and how we can extract a number of Metrics to operate by. We also deep dive into this subject in our Do More Deals Workshops to truly help you establish your own unique set of metrics according to the business model you are operating.

The first big question to understand, which you should already know the answer to is…

What is your business model and how do you make money?

This comes back to what your entry and exit strategies are.

Now before we jump into this section there's something important to highlight. If you don't have any money right now to invest, it's still crucial to complete this section and set metrics. However when setting them I want you to think as if you are the investor. If you can find and attract deals with decent returns, then you effectively have yourself a product that is either sellable, or investable. You can take that product then out to investors to seek the funding necessary in the knowledge that the deal makes enough profit to pay back all parties. Something better than nothing is better than 100% of nothing. Especially if these are some of your first deals.

If You're Planning On Selling

If you are looking to set up a property development company, where your main exit strategy is to SELL property, then your metrics need to be specific to the type of deals that developers carry out.

Here's a couple of examples:

A. Profit On Cost

Profit on Costs is the net profit you expect to make from a deal divided by the total costs of the project.
Profit on Costs = Net Profit / Total Costs

This is important because you can quickly identify how much money in a physical sense you are likely to make from each deal, while also being able to compare this effective investment with other investments.

B. Profit on Gross Development Value (GDV)

This metric looks at the net profit you expect to make from the deal and divides it by the GDV.

Profit on GDV = Net Profit / Gross Development Value

Some people and lenders like to use this metric instead as it helps identify how good the deal is in overall terms factoring in the uplift created from the deal.

An example...

Luke has been a client of mine since 2020 and a key member of the Property Entrepreneurs Club since its inception.

His focus has been to grow a development business that focuses on securing land and existing properties, adding value through conversion or build and selling for profit.

As a full time teacher, his time has certainly been stretched but his attitude and desire to make property successful has been second to none and last year successfully made the step into full time property.

By his own admission this has been fundamentally down to ensuring each deal he has worked on has made good money and been a stepping stone towards his first goal which was to leave the job.

His key metric for doing deals to SELL is:

Minimum 25% Profit of Gross Costs.

What this means is that after all costs associated with the project, he expects to make at least 25% on the overall project spend. This allows for sufficient margin for things outside of his control such as market depreciation or taking longer to sell the units, whilst also offering enough security to any investors as an alternative exit strategy could be to repay their principal loan via a remortgage at 75% of the new value.

The Project

When working together in the early stages we set about setting this key metric, along with others, for which he sourced and completed on the following deal.

He purchased an end of terrace property with potential to obtain planning on the side garden. A precedent had already been set in the area by another developer and so the confidence levels to obtain the planning were high.

There was still a risk but we were able to mitigate that risk via the offer structure and via the fact that the worst case scenario would be to hold the existing property and operate it as a buy-to-let long term hold and still make money.

This project therefore took on two phases.

Phase 1 - Buy house, refurb, obtain planning on the side and sell existing house

Phase 2 - Build out the garden plot (new build) and sell new house

Let's break down the numbers.

£205,000	Purchase Price of House + Garden
£15,000	Refurb Existing House
£10,000	Purchase Costs (Stamp Duty, Legals etc including cost to split the title to separate the garden)
£35,000	Finance Costs on Loans during ownership of Existing House & Paying off JV partner
£5,000	Planning Costs to obtain permission to build in garden
£280,000	**Gross Costs During Phase 1**
£240,000	Sale of Existing House (net of sales costs)
-£40,000	"Profit" from sale (although actually this is the cost to own the garden, i.e. he now owned the garden with planning for £40,000)

The reason Luke approached it in this way was because he borrowed some money to secure the original house from a friend of his. The plan was to always go for planning but if it was rejected he would've remortgaged the house at 75% of the new valuation at £250,000.

Thus raising a new mortgage of £187,500.

With this £187,500 he would pay back his friend back the principal loan of £180,000 plus some of the agreed interest - and would own the house which would rent for £1,350 per month. Thus making Luke approximately £700 per month net cashflow having paid back all initial debts, leaving little money in the deal.

This was a great example of minimising the downside and maximising the upside but because he did obtain planning, he moved into Phase 2. These were the figures:

£40,000	Purchase Cost of Garden (after phase 1)
£120,000	Build New 2-bed House
£35,000	Gross Finance Costs on Development Loan for build costs over term plus all extras / fees
£195,000	Gross Costs of Project
£250,000	Sale of New House (net of sales costs)
£65,000	Net Profit (i.e. money in bank after all costs)

Thus the final metric worked out as:

£65,000 (net profit) / £195,000 (gross costs) = **33.3%**

Not bad for one of Luke's first new build projects. However Luke's mindset throughout this whole project was that this was the learning curve and his opportunity to build momentum in this business. Off the back of this project he has not only learnt a lot, but has also built a network of reliable trades, delivered a positive return to a joint venture partner and investor, and knows which people he can trust and leverage going forward into bigger deals.

If You're Planning On Holding

If you are setting up an investment company where your main exit strategy is to HOLD property, then your metrics need to be different.

A. Return On Capital Employed (ROCE) - same as ROI/ROC/COCR

The return on capital employed is a measure of how much money you make from your investment compared to the amount of actual physical cash left in it. It shows how much profit you're making relative to the cash you invested. It is similar to other terms such as Return On Investment (R.O.I) or Cash on Cash Return (COCR).

Return On Capital Employed (ROCE) = Net Income / Capital Input

There are usually a couple of phases when calculating ROCE.

1. Phase 1, which is based on the returns you would achieve using the funds and finance required for purchase.
2. Phase 2 which assesses the ROCE on any funds left in after you refinance against any uplifted value.

Again how you set your metric will be based upon how you intend to operate and which phase of the growth cycle you are in. If you are looking to grow then you may wish to recycle as much of your money as possible. If you are looking to sustain or pay down debt then your approach may be different. As we are still in the growth phase within my investment company, I look to recycle funds where possible so my ROCE metric is based on the Phase 2 figures. I.e. what my return is on any capital I have left in the deal after I have refinanced.

Let's look at a high level example of how this works with one of my previous deals.

Understanding the situation is key. The plan here was to buy the property which was a 3 bed low lease flat, extend the lease to 125 years and refurb it to a high standard. The exit strategy was to rent it long term on an Assured Shorthold Tenancy (AST).

We purchased the property outright (i.e. with cash), did the necessary uplift works and then refinanced (obtained a new mortgage) after six months against the new uplifted value.

Here's some of the high level numbers:

Phase 1 - purchase of the property using cash and add value

£125,000	Purchase Price including new 125 year lease
£4,000	Closing Costs (inc. SDLT, legals, surveys etc)
£18,000	Refurb Costs
£147,000	**Gross Costs of Project**
£11,700	**Gross Rent per annum**

£10,295	Net Rent per annum (after management fees)
7.00%	**R.O.C.E**

If we left it there in terms of how we financed the purchase using cash - our ROCE would've been around 7% as the full £147,000 cash was utilised.

£10,295 / £147,000 x 100% = 7.00% R.O.C.E

However, since our business model and goal is to grow the portfolio to a certain level, and operate the whole portfolio at a target of 60% Loan-To-Value (LTV) - we are still in the growth phase. So with this property we refinanced to 75% LTV on a five year fixed product.

After 5-10 years the capital appreciation in the area is expected to take the LTV to around the 60% levels. Therefore we are using the market a little bit in our long term planning. Plus this strategy enables us to recycle more cash to do more deals.

Phase 2 - Refinance against new uplifted value to extract funds:

£180,000	New GDV (Gross Development Value) of the 3-bed Flat
£135,000	New Mortgage Balance at 75% LTV
£5,110	New Net Annual Rent (after management costs and new mortgage payments)
£14,500	**Remaining Capital Left In after all costs**
35.2%	**R.O.C.E**

What this deal effectively means is that the £14,500 left in this deal is producing a 35.2% return. At the time of writing our investment business ROCE metric is 30%.

What is great about the ROCE metric is you can now compare this investment vehicle against others offering direct returns on any cash invested. For example if I had £14,500 to my disposal I have a choice of how I invest this in the various investment schemes and products available in the open market. There are very few that can deliver a 35.2% return with the same levels of security as property.

B. Yield

Another good metric to consider, especially if you're planning to hold the property, is the yield. I like to use this one as it's a very simple and quick calculation you can do to determine from a very high level whether a potential investment is worth pursuing, or exploring further.

There are a number of different types of yield calculations you can do but I use Gross Yield. Gross Yield is calculated by dividing the Gross Annual Income by the Gross Project Costs:

Gross yield = Gross Annual Income / Gross Costs

The reason I like to use Gross Yield as a metric in our business is because it's a quick calculation that allows us to sift through potential opportunities quickly. I know for example that if a potential scheme is projecting a 10% Gross Yield, then nine times out of ten, the ROCE will be higher once you remortgage - thus making the ROCE a double digit percentage.

It's not perfect as sometimes a lower projected gross yield can still produce a high ROCE, as the below example shows but it's a good, easy one to get used to. So looking at the same 3 bed flat example from the

ROCE section above. The Gross Yield calculation for this project was:

Gross Income (£11,700) / Gross Costs (£147,000) = Gross Yield (7.96%)

However once we applied leverage (i.e. remortgaged) our ROCE was in excess of 35%.

C. Capital Left In

"Capital Left In" is effectively the amount of money you leave in a deal. This can be at any stage whether you buy in cash and leave it unencumbered (without any debt) or after refinancing and pulling out some of the initial capital invested. This metric is useful particularly for those who are looking to recycle funds as much as possible and perhaps have a limited starting pot.

For example for someone who has a starting pot of say £200,000. The maximum they may be willing to leave in a deal may be £40,000, allowing them to buy five properties using their starting sum.

Capital Left In = Total Initial Investment - Money Out Via Refinancing

For someone who only has £50,000, they may wish to recycle all their funds out. However it is important to recognise that recycling all funds is much trickier these days. In order to recycle all funds, you will need to choose strategies that add enough uplift to the property to achieve the feat. Simply put, the gross costs on a deal (i.e. the total amount of money a deal requires) needs to be 75% or less that the end value in order to recycle all funds.

Is there a specific amount of money that you are comfortable to be left in a deal?

By understanding how much money you are willing to retain in a deal (or an investor if you are working with one), enables you to assess your ability to leverage and continue investing. If all your funds are tied up in one property, you won't have the flexibility to pursue additional opportunities. Therefore, knowing this in advance will help you map out how many deals you can do in what time frame.

D. Cashflow

This refers to the amount of net income you generate each month or year from a deal.

Net Cashflow = Income - Expenses

As you will find, all of these metrics are heavily linked to each other. So whilst on one hand you may find a seemingly great deal whereby you hit all of the three metrics above

1. ROCE is greater than 30%
2. Gross Yield is higher than 10%
3. Capital Left In is less than £40,000

You may not hit this cashflow metric, which is arguably just as, if not more important. The following example shows how you can meet all the three metrics above yet actually make very little money on an ongoing basis. The figures below are theoretical to highlight the issue:

£125,000	Purchase Price
£4,000	Closing Costs (inc. SDLT, legals, surveys etc)
£18,000	Refurb Costs
£147,000	**Gross Costs of Project**
£15,000	**Gross Rent per annum**

£250,000	New GDV (Gross Development Value) of the Property
£187,500	New Mortgage Balance at 75% LTV

-£40,000	**Capital Left In after all costs (i.e. all funds returned plus an additional £40k in the bank)**

£11,250	Mortgage Costs Per Year (at 6% Interest Only)
£1,800	Management Fees (at 12%)
£1,500	Service Charges & Ground Rent
£450	**Cashflow per year**

In this example we have the following metrics:

1. R.O.C.E = Infinite (because we have all our money out)
2. Gross Yield = 10.2%
3. Capital Left In = £0 (in fact we actually have an extra £40k in the bank)

However, we're only making £450 per year. It won't take anything much to go wrong, say a percentage point or two rise in the interest rate or having to fix a faulty boiler for the property to be costing you money each year. A lot of effort and energy for next to no cashflow.

Yet for some, they could argue that they now have an extra £40k in the bank that they didn't before to do more deals with which isn't costing them any money - because the property is covering the cost of that additional finance. Some people might do this, others won't. So it really does depend on your investment strategy.

Setting a minimum cashflow metric therefore may be important to you if your plan is to build a residual income from each asset that is purchased.

So what is your minimum cashflow per property for it to be worthwhile?

Again this will depend on strategy and what you're looking to achieve. For me at the beginning (if you remember) I wanted to make a minimum of £12,000 cashflow per property per year. This was driven by my goal to leave my job at the time.

Having consistent positive cashflow on each project allows you to weather storms in terms of increasing interest rates, fluctuations in property prices or unexpected costs. Even if there's a market downturn, as long as you're still making money, you have a better chance of riding it out and waiting for prices to recover. Plus if you have a primary source of income currently that for whatever reason is taken away from you then you don't have the added stress of having to find cash each and every month to keep your property afloat.

The other thing to be aware of is that if you're not making much regular cashflow and both the property prices decline and interest rates increase, you'll likely find yourself in a difficult situation. You would have to find additional funds from elsewhere to sustain the monthly payments, and may not be in a position to remortgage (if you choose a fixed rate product) which can lead to a chain reaction of financial challenges. This is what happened to many perceivably wealth investors during the 2008 financial crisis. They stacked their portfolios to high in terms of LTV and were not able to refinance when the capital values dropped. So their only options were to sell them at a heavily discounted rate or to be repossessed by the lenders.

Remember all the above metrics are completely based on you, and you should consider where you are starting from and what you're looking to build. As already mentioned, someone with £10m in the bank will likely have completely different objectives and thus metrics, to someone with £100k in the bank.

So take some time to understand how the financials work when structuring deals so you can set metrics within a realistic and reasonable range. If you feel you need some support on the financial engineering and structuring side of things, come and join us at one of our upcoming Property Entrepreneurs Club workshops where we regularly deep dive into this aspect.

Keep It Simple And Get Creative Later

Always remember, keep things simple and avoid overwhelming yourself.

Before you start getting creative and merging strategies, looking at alternative exit strategies and back up plans - it's crucial to have a solid understanding of the process and to have practised the financial engineering behind deals.

It's like building a strong foundation by learning the basic concepts and then implementing them effectively before moving on to more complex strategies. Once you're comfortable with the calculations, inputs, and outputs, you can then explore more creative approaches later on.

CHAPTER 6
DEAL ANALYSIS

Deal analysis is a process we use to analyse deals to see if they meet our target metrics. I often notice two common mistakes when it comes to analysing deals. Some people tend to rush through the process without fully understanding the details, while others get stuck overthinking and analysing to the point of indecision. It's crucial therefore to find the right balance. The most important thing to remember is that deal analysis is there to check if the deal works. By this I mean that the numbers add up and there is sufficient profit margins.

Another reason we do deal analysis is so that we can prove to *others* that the deal works. Often there are a number of stakeholders involved in real estate property transactions such as banks, mortgage providers, investors, business partners or shareholders. It is important therefore to not only be able to prove to yourself that a deal stacks up, but to convince other parties to invest in the deal with you.

This process is also a crucial step in identifying and satisfying yourself with any potential risks the deal may possess. You can identify risks by asking yourself a series of "what if" questions as you go through - here are a handful of said questions:

- What if we don't achieve the projected end value?
- What if the refurb costs come in higher?
- What if the lender wants a higher percentage?
- What if it takes longer than expected to tenant or sell it?

The deal analysis process thus enables you to build in a factor of safety and present potential scenarios for how you would overcome any challenges or risks you may encounter. Therefore not only are you able to prove that the deal works financially, but you are building in risk mitigation at the same time. Plus at the end you will have some hard, black and white data that you can base some key decisions off. For example:

- What else do I need to find out before I can proceed?

- Does this deal project to make a big enough profit?
- Does this deal fit into my wider business plan?
- How much money do I need to raise?
- Can I pay back any investors or lenders?
- Are the risks manageable?

The Two Stages Of Deal Analysis

Think of Deal Analysis as a financial tool or model. Our job is to input various factors and information. Then the model crunches the relevant numbers to give a bunch of results or outputs. It's a machine that is specifically designed to assess whether or not we are likely to make money out of the deal or not.

There are a number of inputs that we need to put into the model such as:

- How much things are going to cost to acquire/control the asset
- How much income will we generate in terms of rent or sales
- How much will it cost on and ongoing basis to operate it (if holding) or through agency fees, etc. (if selling)

The type of outputs that we are aiming to obtain from the process may be:

- Percentage returns (i.e ROCE or Yield metrics - see Chapter 5)
- Profit margins (i.e. Profit on Cost)
- End Valuations (GDVs)

Our job is to:

- Define the inputs
- Define what we want to find out (the outputs)
- Identify risks
- Refine to create the best potential outcome

Once we load this kind of information into the model, it will output the data that we want. When we know our metrics (from Chapter 5), it will then help us make decisions as to whether we want to proceed with the deal or not.

The key is to keep it simple to start with and when we get good at this, we can then start to build additional layers of complexity as we see fit.

A deal analysis model is unique to each of us, based around our goals, metrics and strategies.

We define the inputs and we define the outputs. It is the same fundamental process regardless of which strategy you choose to adopt, the only thing that changes are the inputs and outputs.

The Two Stages and Four Areas Of Deal Analysis

Now we have a basic understanding of what deal analysis is and why we need to do it, let's dive deeper into the process. Let's break it down step by step to understand how this financial model works and how you can build one, unique to you to achieve your desired outcomes.

Firstly the Deal Analysis process is based on two key timeline stages.

1. **Stage 1:** The period of "Control and Readying". Basically the stage of getting the property under your control and getting ready to either tenant or sell.
2. **Stage 2:** The period of "Exit". This is when the property begins to make you money whether via a tenant or sale.

Remembering these two stages is important because the way we analyse returns from deals is based on the amount of money it costs to complete Stage 1 vs the amount of money we make in Stage 2.

Let's put some meat on the bone now and dive into the Deal Analysis process which is split into four main areas.

1. **Capital Requirements (Stage 1)**

The first aspect to consider is the capital requirements. This involves understanding the amount of money we need to get this deal under control during Stage 1 from a chronological point of view.

This includes the price we agree with the seller to either buy the property, or get it under control - we might be doing a rent to rent deal structure whereby we only pay an upfront deposit and first month's rent - so we're not buying it but controlling it.

We will also want to include any costs such as Stamp Duty, legal fees, surveys etc., along with any other expenses such as financial costs and "getting the property ready" costs such as refurbishment/build costs.

The capital requirements therefore refer to the total amount of money needed to set up and get the property up and running.

I like to make subsections within Capital Requirements to cover the following:

A. Control Costs - How much is it going to cost to control?

This is all about taking control of the property, which means understanding how much it will cost to acquire it (if that's the strategy). This may include the total purchase price agreed with the seller, legal fees, stamp duty etc. In simpler terms, it refers to the total amount of money needed to pay in order to become the rightful owners/controllers of the property. Some items that fall into this subsection would be:

- Purchase Price
- Stamp Duty
- Legal Fees (this could be combined or split out to include each individual disbursement, searches, telegraphic bank transfer fees, vat etc)
- Finders Fees
- Upfront Surveys (homebuyers, structural, asbestos, etc.)

B. Finance Costs - How much is it going to cost upfront and in interest until exit?

This involves understanding how much it will cost to secure the necessary funding for the transaction. Not everyone will buy outright in cash, so if borrowing is required in the form of a mortgage then this will most likely come with fees (broker fees, arrangement fees, surveys, valuations etc.) Also if there is a refurb or build to do, which will take a number of months then we need to account for the period where there will be no income until the property is income producing ready. So the ongoing cost of the interest payments need to be factored in at this stage. Some items that may fall into this subsection could be:

- Broker Fees
- Arrangement Fees
- Valuation Fees
- Independent Legal Advice fees (relevant if obtaining finance via a Ltd Company)
- Loan Exit Fees
- Interest Costs for duration between picking up keys and exit (sell or rent)

The finance costs relate to the expenses incurred when obtaining a loan and all the associated costs, such as interest payments and additional fees, to *acquire* control of the property.

C. Ready To Exit Costs

This refers to the expenses associated with preparing the property for potential sale or rental. It includes costs such as refurbishment expenses, expenses related to finding tenants, and any ongoing costs during the refurbishment period. For example this may include (but not limited to):

- Build costs
- Planning Costs and fees
- Professional fees (architects, engineers, party wall surveyors etc)
- Utilities & rates for duration of build
- Licensing costs
- Guarantees & warrantees
- Insurances
- Tenant find fees
- Staging and Marketing costs

To summarise, the capital requirements are divided into three subsections that help understand the total costs involved in acquiring, financing, and preparing the property for potential exit. You will not know every single figure to the penny, so it is important to put an allowance or budget in there for the time being. You can circle back round at a later date to update these allowances with more accurate figures. With experience these allowances start to become more accurate.

However when you use allowances it is important to then carry out further research to find out whether that budget is realistic and achievable. Perhaps you've allowed £5,000 for architect fees. The next logical step would then be to obtain specific quotes from a number of architects for that particular project to confirm accuracy.

2. <u>Income (Stage 2)</u>

Let's move on to the second element, which is understanding how much money we are going to make from the deal. This is where we move into Stage 2 in terms of the chronology of the deal. We have now spent everything to set the property up and we are now in the money making stage.

The inputs at this point will depend on our main exit strategy. If it is to HOLD, i.e rent the property out, then we need to determine how much rent we can charge for it. Equally, if our strategy is to SELL, then we need to know its selling price as accurately as possible.

Knowing both however regardless of our exit strategy is necessary as we can explore different exit strategies and make informed decisions about the financial potential of the deal. If we plan to Hold, knowing how much the property is going to be worth after any uplift will enable us to work out how much we can borrow against the new valuation.

Here are two ways to work out how much the property will be worth:

A. Research comparables and build in a factor of safety

You can conduct research on similar properties in your local area. Look for properties that are comparable to what you plan to create, such as rental rooms or one or two-bedroom flats. Check out properties within a quarter to half-mile radius and see what prices they are offering.

At the end of the day a property is only worth what someone is willing to pay for it - this applies in both a sales and rental market. So establishing what else is on the market is important because when faced with a decision, a buyer or renter will compare properties and see what they can get for their money.

This is also why we see cycles in terms of valuations and rentals in property. In a rising market, people selling or renting their properties will push the value up in order to maximise their returns. When someone agrees to proceed at that higher value it establishes a new high in terms of what a comparable property would sell/rent for in the area. The same effect happens in a dropping market as buyers/renters try to undercut on the price they are willing to pay, which in turn sets the new comparable price at a lower level. Supply and demand also plays a big part in this cycle.

When looking to estimate end valuations and rentals it is important to build in a factor of safety based on what market we are currently in, or what *might* happen in the future. The magnitude of this factor of safety is a personal choice and is something for you to play around with. The reason we do this is because there is always a good period of time between agreeing a deal with a vendor, to completing the purchase (if buying), then adding value (if that's the plan), and exiting. If holding and refinancing, then usually you need to own the property for a minimum of six months before most lenders will look to offer you a new mortgage. During this time, the market could turn and start reducing. That's where a factor of safety comes in handy. On the flip side, if the market goes up, then your factor of safety has just created additional profit than what you were expecting. Win-win.

If looking to work with investors particularly to help raise funds for projects, some investors will like seeing you build in some contingency for potential market conditions. It shows an understanding of market risk.

B. Speak to agents, surveyors & other owners/investors

Don't be afraid to pick up the phone and speak to local agents and ask for assistance. They can help you with the research process by providing their expertise and giving you price estimates. You can call two or three agents and ask them questions like, "What rental or sale prices can I expect for properties like mine once they're ready?" Since agents are familiar with the area and regularly value properties, they can offer guidance.

However it's important to understand that agents are understandably going to want to attract your business in return for helping you out. So they may inflate the price a touch in order to do so. I'm not saying every agent is the same, because they are not, but this is why speaking with a few is great and taking an average of the figures supplied.

Additionally, consider connecting with other property owners and investors in your area. Networking is key here. Join relevant Facebook groups or other online communities where local investors gather. Engage with them and don't be afraid to ask direct questions to obtain direct answers.

By doing this, you can tap into the experiences and knowledge of others who have already ventured into similar projects. There's no better data than actual, real life figures from someone actually doing it. Buy them coffee, or lunch or offer to help them out with anything you can in return for helping you out.

C. Use Online Data Tools & Work on a Price per Square Meter / Foot Basis

Much of property valuations from a sales and rental perspective is done on size. Therefore establishing what other comparable properties are worth on a "per square foot" basis (or " per square metre" if you're more 21st century) then you can apply an average rate to your property to estimate an end value.

There are useful online tools that can help with this that compile large volumes of recent sales and listed price data to establish average rates for square foot. They each have a cost but can often be worth every penny as they save a lot of time. You can use portals, floorplans and the EPC register to work things out manually, but it can be time intensive.

I will touch on the benefits of working more on a "per square foot basis" a little later.

3. <u>Costs During Exit (Inputs)</u>

The final element to consider in terms of the inputs into our deal analysis model are the costs incurred during the *exit*. Here this is about understanding and allowing for all the costs that will only be incurred once you have triggered your preferred exit, i.e. whether you are renting or selling.

In other words, it's important to understand that there are costs associated with actually making the money from the deal which are only relevant to the exit you choose.

If you intend to sell for example, these expenses may include things like:

- Agency fees
- Solicitor fees
- Indemnities

If you intend to hold and rent out the property, you may want to include things like:

- Agency management fees,
- Ongoing tenant finding fees,
- Utility bills (if you include them in the rent),
- Maintenance expenses (I use a percentage allowance),
- Voids (potential periods when the property may be vacant).

Which of these will be relevant depends on the strategy you choose so if you intend to set up short lets, you will also have costs of linen, regular cleaning costs, gardening and costs for platforms such as Airbnb for any bookings that you take.

This section can also be divided into a few sub-categories:

A. **Bills** - These are the things that are going to cost you while managing and operating the rental property but obviously are very strategy specific. These costs may include:

- Utility bills (such as electricity, gas and water bills)
- Broadband and phone lines

- Insurance
- Council taxes (if you are responsible for paying)

B. **Management Fees** - Again depending on how you intend to manage your portfolio if you are going to outsource or insource this I would always make an allowance for this. You may expect to pay around 8 to 15% of the gross rental income to outsource management to an external letting agent. It's important to remember to include VAT (Value Added Tax) as most agencies are VAT rated.

C. **Maintenance & Voids** - Again very specific to your strategy and how you intend to set up your contracts in terms of responsibilities. You would however most likely want to make some allowance for some ongoing repairs and maintenance, as well as an allowance to cover any periods when the property is vacant and not generating rental income between tenancies.

4. <u>Returns & Refinance (Outputs)</u>

Your outputs are effectively a set of equations that you define based upon what you wish to work out from your analysis. This is where you'll want to go back to your metrics that you identified in the previous chapter.

As you become more familiar with the figures and how they relate to each other you can start to get creative and build additional layers to your model. However as eluded to already, start simple and build from there.

The key thing to achieve from this whole process is to actually *understand* the process. Once you do that, you have armed yourself with the most important skill in property, which is the "financial engineering". You can then start applying this across lots of different sectors and strategies and when you really start to spot opportunities.

Pricing Per Square Foot / Metre

Starting to think and work on a "per square foot" basis can become very impactful to your business. As you become more experienced you can work out approximate buying costs, build costs and end valuations all on a "per square foot" or "square metre" basis. For example:

1. If you know that in your local area the approximate resale rate for a house is say £5,000 per square metre.
2. A refurbishment rate is around £1,750 per square metre (including all costs of finance, fees etc).
3. Your profit on cost metric is 25%.

4. Then you need to be buying a property at less than £2,000 per square metre in order to make a good profit.

£5,000 x 25% = £1,250 (this is our profit margin)
£5,000 - £1,250 - £1,750 (build rate) = £2,000

Therefore…

1. If you could buy a 500 sqm office at less than £1,000,000 to turn into residential units.
2. It should cost you around £875,000 in costs to convert.
3. Be worth around £2,500,000, and
4. Make you around £625,000 profit.

Very rough and ready, but this now gives you a good indication on what to look for and in what areas.

PART 3
POSITION

CHAPTER 7
DEAL TRIANGLE

The Three Things That Must Come Together in Property Deals

Now we are building the understanding with regards to the financial engineer behind property deals, and have built ourselves a business plan based upon the Three M's. We are in a position to start implementing. This is the fun bit, and for most a crucial step as some people will push on from here and move the needle in a big way, or will keep going around in circles.

This Chapter is all about one thing: Positioning.

Positioning yourself within your marketplace is not just important, it's absolutely pivotal to the speed in which you move that needle and start seeing genuine results. Much of this comes back to your mindset, as discussed in Chapter 1 but now armed with a solid business plan and a good understanding of the financials, you should also have some clarity and confidence to back yourself up with.

It is now you can ask yourself the question - Why Me?

Or better still, with the business hat on - Why Us?

Why would anyone, whether that be estate agents, investors, vendors etc., want to do business with you? You should know the answer already but now is the time to put that into words.

Positioning is something we are always doing, but for many people it is *without* purpose. When I started in property I was clearly positioning myself in a particular way, which led to a few decent deals early on. Then I lost my way a little bit as I became distracted. This lack of clarity had a major impact on how I was subconsciously positioning myself.

Having realised the errors of my ways, and re-calibrating as I did, I started to position myself with a lot more purpose. Saying certain things, in a certain way to help build credibility and authority - more on this in Chapter 8.

Whilst results didn't arrive overnight, it is no surprise that I started to attract the type of opportunities that I really wanted. More agents sent me more deals. More people approached me with particular situations that they wanted some help with. These often led to joint-ventures or opportunities to jump into deals. Investors reached out to me asking if they could work with me and all of these new doors of opportunities just continued to snowball to the point where I had to start saying no to people.

But this is where I learnt another big lesson... Saying yes to every opportunity that is presented to you can actually work against you.

Saying yes to everything can lead to issues of its own such as:

1. Creating overwhelm - fighting fires on multiple fronts and trying to juggle several balls all at once can be daunting and lead to burnout.
2. Losing clarity all over again - if you say yes to everything you can lose clarity over your original purpose and you can often be led down different paths and away from your original goals.
3. Not being remembered for anything specific - when you say yes all the time it's difficult to

define who you are and what people think of you for. When people need help with a problem they go to a niched expert, not a generalist.

That is why having your business plan and ***sticking to it*** is so important, because now you can do two things:

1. Know how to position yourself to attract the opportunities *you* want.
2. Know which opportunities to push forward with and which to pass on.

The Deal Triangle

During a period of self-reflection and redefinition back in 2017, I had a massive realisation.

I realised that in property, there are always three things that *must* come together in order for any type of property deal to happen. Without any one of these three things the whole thing fails and deals stop dead in their tracks.

This is when The Deal Triangle™ was born.

The deal triangle consists of three essential elements that influence the success of any deal:

1. The DEAL itself (i.e. the vehicle that is going to make a profit),
2. The CAPABILITY of the person/team responsible for creating or extracting that profit (experience/knowledge), and
3. The MONEY.

Without any one of these things, the deal will always fail. You could also think of it like a three legged stool, take one leg away and the whole thing falls over.

Why Is This Fundamentally Important?

Knowing these three things becomes incredibly powerful because you can now leverage each one to attract others. For example, we know that in order to make money in property we need to be doing deals - ideally lots of them.

But if you don't have access to any deals how could you start attracting them?

Well, by positioning yourself in your market as either someone with money, or someone with capability. Or better still, both.

"But Tanner, what if I don't have any of the three things in the Deal Triangle?"

Well, remember we know that each of the three things attracts the other two. So whilst you may feel as though you don't have any of them right now, it's all about *perception*. It's about making others *think* you do.

Think of it like a drop shipping company - and let's call this company "Tan's Toys Ltd".

An online dropshipping company in its simplest form, literally consists of a website where people can buy products. However, being a dropshipping company, Tan's Toys Ltd doesn't own any of its stock, it is simply an intermediary. So when someone comes along and buys a toy, Tan's Toys Ltd gets on the blower to the supplier of said toy and orders it to be shipped directly from the manufacturer to the end user.

Property is exactly the same. As Property Entrepreneurs we are intermediaries pulling together all the pieces of the puzzle, just like a dropshipping company does. And just like a dropshipping company, we need to advertise the fact that we have *access* to the stock. Which in our case is either the... money, deals or capability.

There Is Always Someone On The Other Side

The other thing to realise here is that there is always someone on the other side of the triangle, seeking one or two of the other things.

People are always out there positioning themselves as:

- "Sourcers" (i.e. they have deals),
- "Investors" (i.e. they have money) or
- "Service Providers" (i.e they have some capability and knowledge of property).

Yet they aren't necessarily aware of Deal Triangle, so you can use this to your advantage and position yourself accordingly.

Deals First Or Money First?

Let's dive into each element briefly.

1. First element: Deals (i.e. the Product)

The property industry has created this Chicken and Egg debate as to which comes first, deals or money. Some people assume that once they have access to money, deals will naturally follow but I don't think this is true - there's a lot more to it. On the flip side, if you have a deal, and I mean a properly considered and profitable deal then money will *definitely* follow.

Deals are the foundation because they are effectively the product in which people are seeking and for which make people money. Doing deals also builds momentum, attracts more money and builds experience and capability. Without them, there is no momentum, no experience and no money being made.

There are a lot of people you can tap into who can provide you deals, and who would be highly interested in discussing ways to work together. Perhaps think about who you know, or need to know to start gaining access to more deals?

Estate agents' whole business model for example is about connecting sellers of properties with buyers of properties. Usually they have substantial marketing resources specifically targeting sellers and are skilled at negotiating. They are fundamentally driven by one thing, completions - no completions = no money. Their pain points are usually the number of transactions that fall through, and the time it takes for transactions to complete. So consider this for a moment... If you were to position yourself as a credible buyer with access to loads of cash who was able to complete transactions quickly - do you think estate agents would be interested in sending you some deals?

Of course they would. In Chapter 9 I talk more about working with agents and how to effectively turn local estate agents into your personal sourcing agents.

But agents are not the only people with access to deals. There are thousands of other property entrepreneurs always looking for deals so ask yourself how could you access those opportunities? Well maybe attending regular networking events and positioning yourself as someone with money and capability??

2. Second element: Money (Finance)

Every deal needs money, whether it be £1 or £10 million. Often however people see their lack of money as an impassable stumbling block to doing more deals. As we've just covered, good deals attract the necessary funding - and there is more money out there in this World than there ever has been before. Each and every day more and more people are coming into significant wealth and they don't know what to do with it.

The key is to understand how people think about money, and who are the types of people who may be interested in funding your property venture or working with you as a funding partner. I've found that there are a few different types of people in this world when it comes to money.

1. The Scared

There are more and more stories out there in the media of people being shafted and losing money in XYZ investment schemes - whether it's the latest crypto failure, property investment gone bad or ponzi scheme. As a result a lot of people just don't know who to trust anymore. So instead of doing anything, they just sit on their hands and leave their cash in the bank doing nothing. These people are very risk averse and so are hard to convince to work with you. They require a lot of education in terms of how their money will be kept safe and you have to put in a lot of legwork to build the trust. But if you can work on this and provide lots of confidence to them (via your perceived capability and experience) then they may be open to testing the water with you on a small scale before becoming a long term trusted investor. Usually however, these are long burners and I try to focus on the other types of people as follows.

2. *The Busy*

These people are either professionals working in high flying jobs that pay well or run successful businesses but put big demands on their time. They understand money and the importance of investing but thinking about how, where and who to invest their money with can be a stress they would rather not deal with. These people understand the power of leverage and are more likely to be open to discussions with you about how you can help them "get into property".

3. *The Unaware*

These people simply don't know what to do with their money. Some are perhaps working with an Independent Financial Advisor who is investing their money for them in the markets (who are most often not independent, and often charge hefty fees). Some may have money sitting in bank accounts not doing much. Some may have pensions that they didn't realise they could access and invest into property. I have met a number of people who are sitting on some serious wealth, but just simply don't know how to get it working for them.

The Busy and The Unaware are prime potential investors in your business. All they need is for someone to show them the light and show them what is possible in property - and of course, that's where you come in.

3. Third Element: Capability (Knowledge & Experience)

Consider this scenario: Imagine you encounter someone who happens to possess a significant surplus of wealth. They're in a position where they're eager to invest and make use of their resources. You approach them with a compelling deal yet you don't really come across as someone who really knows what they're doing. Ask yourself, what are the odds that this individual would work with you? I suspect it is quite low.

However, the potential for them to invest or contribute money to your venture becomes remarkably higher when there is trust in place regarding your capabilities. No matter how good a deal someone has, it is very difficult to convince someone to invest unless there is a good level of trust in the individuals involved. This is why showcasing your capability and understanding about the property market is so important.

Walk The Talk

To build solid trust and showcase your capability to deliver successful deals you need to be able to walk the talk. The key is on positioning yourself in a way that shows others that you are actually doing. Taking action, learning, taking risks and not afraid to put yourself out there. Being part of communities and networks also helps to showcase that you are being active within the property space. You turn up and will continue turning up come rain or shine.

It's crucial to be actively involved and to be seen actively participating in the property industry. Not being afraid to promote yourself and showcase what you are doing. Attending networking meetings regularly, engaging in only forums, and investing into masterminds opens so many doors. It proves that you are an action taker rather than someone who loves the idea of doing projects.

Be Consistent

Being consistent in your message and your attendance at industry events demonstrates your commitment to the cause. I run a lot of networking and training events and the number of people I meet who attend only once, and then you never see them again is quite high. Those who keep coming back build better relationships with others and the level of trust goes up. It also naturally draws attention from other investors who see your consistency. Don't be a flash in the pan.

Be Confident

I remember a good number of years ago, when I had only been in property a couple of years, I was very shy when it came to self promotion. The classic "Why Me?" question would often crop up in my mind. Why would anyone be interested in what I have to say?

I would often feel as though I was never knowledgeable enough, or experienced enough to standing up at a networking event, or posting about my property journey on social media. There was always that fear that someone more experienced would shoot me down, or correct me for saying something wrong. So I would just stay quiet.

However it wasn't until a good few years into my property journey that I realised that this was totally holding me back. The fear of what *might* happen was actively suffocating my ability to push forward and grow. I decided to push myself out of my comfort zone and started posting "progress" photos of active projects online.

I then also approached the organiser of one of the local property networking events and asked if I could help in running, promoting and growing the event.

Within a few short months of doing these two things, I had investors approaching me for advice. I had people asking if they could get involved in my projects and I even sold a project to a local investor and made a cool £5,000 for doing so. Which at the time was a nice little bonus.

I always held my personal reputation as one of the highest priorities in life. Ensuring everyone thinks good of me and being careful to not upset anyone. However I realised a good while back that whilst this can be a good value to have, it can also massively work against you if you're not careful.

Giving too much of a shit about what people thought of me, stopped me from positioning myself better and doing some of the things that I needed to do to grow my business and reputation. Having self confidence to put yourself out there, deal with any situations that head your way and pushing yourself forward is fundamental.

Fake It 'Til You Make It

Now let's address a big elephant in the room and the one that most people don't have the cajones to admit.

That is, every so often you just have to take that self-confidence and fake it 'til you make it.

Business is a people's game, and people need convincing. So whilst I don't ever advocate being a complete liar or fraud, don't be afraid to sail a little close to the wind sometimes.

Understand the art of influence and do not be afraid to tell people what *can* be done. Look at it like this...

If you are standing in front of a crowd of starving hungry people, who would quite literally bite your arm off and they were chanting for burgers - what would you do?

Being an entrepreneur I would spot the opportunity and I would sell them a burger there and then. I may not have ever sold burgers before, know how to cook them, or even have any burgers on me.

But I would tell people what *could* be done and figure it out. If someone else can do it, or has done it, then why can't I?

When Elon Musk started Tesla, he took millions of pre-orders from buyers before they even had a fully working prototype. They didn't even have a factory capable of building or delivering any of the orders! He simply convinced people that he could deliver, took their money and figured it out. Tesla has gone on to become one of the most valuable companies in the world.

So if you are speaking to someone with money, and they show an interest in what you are doing in property - make sure you feed them what they want.

Tell them you can help them by working with them and *how* it could work.

Don't be afraid of failing because the only way to fail 100% of the time is to never take any risks or any actions in the first place.

£250,000 in One Day - The Deal Triangle in Action

Back in 2017, I secured three property deals in one day. Of which I made just shy of £250,000 from.

At the time, I had very little cash in the bank (I had just lost close to £50,000 in a failed business venture - a story for another time) however I understood the power of The Deal Triangle.

My theory was if I could find and secure a good deal, then I would be able to raise the money. However in order to secure those good deals I needed to convince estate agents and vendors that I was in a proceedable position.

I did some online research and did quick high level deal analysis on a few properties. I found three potential properties that ticked my criteria - they all met my metrics so I arranged a block viewing on all three and headed out for the afternoon.

At the viewings, I used the techniques covered in Chapter 9 about positioning myself with the agents. I told them I had money burning a hole in my pocket and that I worked with a number of wealthy clients that were looking for good deals.

Neither of which were 100% true at the time - I certainly didn't have money burning a hole in *my* pocket, but I knew that if these deals stacked up well then I *backed myself* to find someone who did.

I took a risk.

That risk then turned into an even bigger one as when I made good offers on all three (where the projected profits were *really* good) - all three were accepted!

My positioning techniques - leveraging the Deal Triangle as someone with Money and Capability - and my knowledge of how to analyse and structure deals worked.

I had myself three very good "products" which I could now leverage to position myself to attract the money I needed. This is when the work really started.

I reached out to everyone I knew who might have money. I started with close friends and family. Then cast the net a little wider via social media and through networking events. I kept the agents in the loop and instructed my solicitors to begin the conveyancing process, however I told them upfront that it might not be me who ends up buying as *"I need to speak to some of my clients and business partners."*

Within a couple of months, I had found an investor at the local networking event that I helped organise to take on one of the deals (that's the £5k I mentioned earlier). My sister and brother in law purchased the second one - of which I charged a sourcing fee and project management fee (discounted of course).

Then I raised some capital from wider family members on a fixed rate loan basis to purchase the third one for myself.

This was when my property business kicked up a notch and when I really started to move the needle. Off the back of these three deals I then started a refurbishment and building company which carried out the refurb work, and has since in its own right gone on to have its own successes, opening further doors of opportunity.

This is when The Deal Triangle™ came to my mind and I started sketching it out.

I basically leveraged the appearance of having Money and Capability to attract Deals. Then when I had Deals, re-positioned myself and leveraged that to attract the Money I needed.

Positioning yourself accordingly can fundamentally change your entire trajectory in property and business. Have some confidence behind your approach, don't be afraid to take some risks and back yourself.

People need convincing and people will only be convinced to work with you if you give them the Deals that will make them money and the confidence in your Capability to deliver those deals successfully.

At your next networking event, try standing up and telling people in the room that you have a few hundred thousand pounds burning a hole in your pocket and you need deals. Let me know on social media what happens...

PART 4
PROMOTE

CHAPTER 8
ATTRACTING OPPORTUNITIES THROUGH SELF-PROMOTION

When it comes to promoting yourself as an experienced property professional, there are a lot of different ways that you can do this. Promotional strategies go beyond just listing achievements, posting on social media or trying to sell yourself at every opportunity. It's about identifying who you are targeting, building an element of excitement and most importantly building trust. I see a lot of people trying every platform and strategy all at once - targeting every man and his dog, without moving the needle. So taking a moment to plan this stuff out and forming a strategy is useful.

When I refer to *promotion,* I mean putting yourself into certain environments to increase both your *visibility* and your *credibility* in your particular field - property. It's about being seen on a consistent basis and building a brand around you and your business. This may involve stepping out of your comfort zone, if this feels foreign to you naturally, and putting yourself in situations that may not feel 100% comfortable at first. But that's OK, discomfort is a sign of growth, and you'll learn from those experiences and feel empowered to develop further.

We are rarely taught how to promote ourselves - especially us Brits. We are a particularly self-deprecating and introverted nation so the idea of *shouting from the rooftops* can make many people's insides churn. But as an entrepreneur you'll know, if no one knows who you are, no one is going to do business with you. The most important thing is to take action, not be afraid of what someone *might* say, and build some momentum.

Imagine you are in the process of hiring a piano tutor for your child.

Would you be more inclined to connect and work with Person A, who is readily discoverable online, talks about their experience in the music industry, shares photos of themselves participating in relevant industry events, and publishes success stories of current and previous students?

Or would you be more likely to approach Person B , who lacks any visible credentials but suggested they can play piano and could help you out?

Person A has showcased some social proof that what they do works, and could work for your child. They have also reminded regularly that they are there and by doing so has built intrigue and trust with you.

Person B on the other hand - how would you even know they existed without any kind of presence, self promotion or proof that they can even do what they said they can?

Time to have a little review about what you are doing right now to increase your visibility?

If you are putting yourself out there, how much success is this bringing? What exactly are you spending time on when it comes to self promotion?

If you are not putting yourself out there much, what could start doing differently for people to discover you?

You Need More Credibility

There's a direct link between how much credibility you have and the opportunities you get access to. So what exactly does credibility mean for a property professional like yourself?

It means that people believe in your expertise and experience, they consider you a reliable source of information and want to know you, or work with you as a trusted partner. Remember the Deal Triangle from the previous Chapter?

Having credibility shows that you've put in the work to understand your industry, and others respect your opinions and insights. It's about being recognised as "one of the good guys" and that you're not another one of those tire-kicking wannabe course junkies. However building credibility takes time so don't delay this stuff.

When you start to combine increased visibility (putting yourself out there) with credibility building then opportunities start dropping in your lap. I am regularly self promoting and putting myself out there. I carry out a lot of different promotional tasks to actively grow my personal brand as I know the power of being seen consistently. For example, I attend, speak at and organise regular events within the industry. I post regularly on social media and actively engage in industry specific groups.

At a networking event recently, I had a 90-second conversation with a local estate agent, if that. We exchanged a few niceties and contact details, and a few weeks later I received a message from him out of the blue. He said he had bumped into a professional sportsperson who wanted to get more involved in property. My name was dropped into the conversation and we were connected by the agent. We jumped on a quick Zoom call a few weeks later and I am now regularly in touch with a Champions League level football player. This person is actively looking to grow his property portfolio and we are working together to support him with that. It's amazing how such a significant opportunity arose from a brief encounter lasting less than a few minutes.

Had I not been at this event in the first place then this estate agent would certainly not have made the connection. But crucially, of all the people who were at the networking event, I was chosen because of the way I positioned myself and built credibility at this event.

Have you ever considered how much it could be worth to you if you were to focus more energy over the coming months, and beyond, just on enhancing your visibility and credibility?

The one meeting I mention above has the potential to be worth millions and this is just one scenario. Property and business is all about people at the end of the day. The key takeaway here is to realise that visibility can bring you significant benefits, and by doing it well, whether through social media, networking or other avenues, you can seriously elevate your credibility within the industry and set yourself apart from others.

So let me ask you a question - what is your desired outcome from boosting your visibility? Is it primarily about financial gain? Is it to secure and do more deals? Or perhaps your aim is to meet some wealthy individuals or partners who you can work with long term? Maybe it is all of the above?

The goal of this chapter is to break down some of the best strategies for boosting your visibility, credibility and fundamentally your access to more opportunities so you can start implementing some of these right away.

Social Media

Let's start here with arguably the easiest and cheapest platform out there.

There really is no excuse these days for not having ways to reach people from all four corners of the globe. While there are several social media options, it's important to underscore that you don't need to be on every single one. Some social media advisors might push for a constant presence on every platform, but let's be realistic. Being everywhere is unnecessary. Instead, focus on making an impact in one or two areas that connects you with your target audience.

So who is your target audience? Think back to Chapter 7 and the different types of people - The Scared, The Busy, The Unaware.

LinkedIn for example holds particular value in the property sector and proves to be an excellent platform for connecting with potential investors. Users of this platform tend to be professionals (The Busy).

Facebook and Instagram are also effective due to their extensive reach. Facebook groups are filled with very specific types of people who have self-certified themselves as interested in specific topics. So these offer free and very targeted access to groups of people who have all shown interest in property, or investing.

What Social Media Posts To Share

Navigating social media can be daunting, especially if you're unsure about the type of posts that will effectively highlight your expertise. No need to overthink and get stuck in analysis-paralysis.

Simply share your personal experiences, values, and even mistakes or moments from your life that you've learnt from. This humanises your brand, making it relatable and approachable. Trying to convince people you never make mistakes and are a perfect fountain of knowledge is unrealistic and hard to keep up.

It's this mixture of expertise and authenticity that makes a deeper connection with people, positioning you as a trusted and influential person.

I've broken down a few different types of posts that you can start utilising that will start increasing your visibility and credibility.

1. Competence

These posts serve as a platform to demonstrate not only your expertise but the fact that you're actually doing it - you are walking the walk.

They may encompass a range of content, including property listings that highlight your portfolio, testimonials from satisfied clients or partners, stories of your successful deals, or a summary of what you learnt at a recent event.

It's effectively a high level CV and an opportunity to showcase your track record to prove to others that you're someone who actually gets on with things. It's essential to foster the belief that you're a dynamic individual capable of managing a number of projects and building a successful business.

It's not all about showcasing deals so if you don't have any property specific projects to showcase, then think about what else you could utilise. There are many transferable skills in property and business so have you had any specific experiences in life that showcases certain types of competence?

These could include conversations you've had, training you've attended, professional bodies you're part of; articles you've written or read; industry events you've recently been to, people you have worked with and would vouch for you as an individual.

Perhaps you could take a picture of this book, share how many deals your business expects to do this year and if anyone would like to be part of your growth then to drop you a direct message?

2. Knowledge Sharing

These posts are all about sharing value. Things you've learnt, or the way you think about things. This is where you can stamp some uniqueness and authority on certain things. Remember, most information and knowledge is already out there, so no one is expecting you to come up with anything completely new. Just your take on things and disseminating the pieces of information that you feel are relevant and useful.

You can also align these posts with specific outcomes that you want to achieve. For instance, if you're seeking investors for deals, you could provide insights into how to effectively utilise funds. Or how hands off investors are able to make money via property transactions. Posts about how inflation is eating money sat in the bank, or how making your money move can lead to compound growth etc.

I'm sure if you sat down for just half an hour and brainstormed all the different bits of information and knowledge you could share, you would come up with enough ideas to last a good while.

If you're unsure about where to start, consider sharing your personal journey. For instance, you might want to post "The Three Most Valuable Property Lessons I've Learned This Month."

If you've read something you disagreed with, let people know.

If you've gained insightful tips from a property book, you could snap a photo of the book and caption it with "I came across this book recently and found a valuable tip about..." This approach effectively conveys your continuous learning all while offering valuable insights for other people to learn from you.

A big part of it is having the confidence to disseminate any information and impart some of your knowledge. Don't be afraid of any negative comments or kick back. There are trolls out there, but they don't matter anywhere near as much as your success.

Do, learn, adapt, do again.

As you begin to perfect these types of posts they will naturally evolve into bigger and better value-bombs that people will follow you and thank you for. Eventually leading to opportunities.

3. Lifestyle

This is your chance to give your intended audience a special insight into your world, making your brand relatable on a personal level. By sharing bits of your daily life and personal experiences, you're not just a property professional; you become a real person connecting with real people.

You can share snippets of your personal life - whether it's a trip to another country, moments with your family, or even a photo of you enjoying your favourite hobby. Often, personal posts like birthday wishes or anniversary celebrations receive more engagement than business-related content.

If you're seeking funding, individuals tend to invest in people they genuinely like and trust. Thus, the more they can discover about you before an actual meeting, the higher the likelihood that they will establish that trust well in advance. Plus it gives you a much easier route to build rapport with them when you do speak directly as you can discuss shared interests or experiences.

Being personable is far more effective than someone who constantly appears overly professional, mechanical, and tough to resonate with. Don't get me wrong, professionalism is important, however an emotional connection matters more. From an investors', business partners, or property owners perspective, looking after them is more paramount. For some, being too formal and "businessy" can put people off as they may perceive you to be more interested in the performance of your business, rather than the performance of their money, assets or interests.

The more they're convinced that you're committed to ensuring their well-being, and that you are more like them, the more trust you build.

It's Not A Popularity Contest

When it comes to social media, just remember it is not all about being the most liked or having the most followers. Many people tend to associate social media with popularity but it's definitely not about that.

You do not have to be followed by thousands of people for social media to be effective. What truly matters is having followers of good quality. People who are engaged and who are actually your target audience.

Engagement Is Most Important

Social media is all about engagement. The more comments and likes that you can get on each post the higher the algorithms will rate you. This means more people will see your future posts. So when you are planning out posts then often simple questions asking people what they have for dinner, or what they think of certain ideas or topics can help increase engagement.

The Hidden Followers

You'll be surprised who is lurking in the background watching and listening and for how long they would do that for. Over the years I have had people approach me after two or three years of following me online. They never engaged in any posts but have just been following. Out of the blue they would reach out to me because they all of a sudden have an immediate need for support.

Having regular Calls to Action within your posts also offers people the opportunity to connect with you outside of social media taking those people from social media into your own personal contact database.

Public Speaking

A common misconception is that public speaking is reserved for educators, trainers, and "gurus". However, I'm going to shatter that notion right away. Public speaking isn't confined to just coaches and mentors; it's a powerful tool you can use to elevate your brand.

The transformation that happens when you're attending a networking event versus being a speaker is huge. It's the shift from being an audience member to becoming a credible leader. Why does this matter so much? Because it positions you in a different way to everyone else in the room. You have stepped up as someone who is willing to share some valuable insights and who knows their stuff.

As you step onto that stage, whether physical or virtual, you're not just sharing information, you're building likability, trust, and sharing your values. A perfect credibility cocktail as already mentioned above. Potential clients, partners, and investors are much more likely to take notice and trust your insights.

Not a public speaking kind of person?

Well public speaking doesn't necessarily mean addressing a stadium full of people. It could be speaking to just one or more individuals. Small networking events, Facebook Lives, Instagram Lives, or even podcasts where you are usually just chatting to one person.

Podcasts, for instance, are an exceptional avenue for sharing knowledge and podcasts can reach potentially thousands of listeners across the globe. Yet there isn't any stage fright or big audiences to worry about. This exposure can lead to more connections, more deals, and more opportunities.

When reaching out to become a public speaker or a podcast guest, it's essential to emphasise the value you can provide to the audience. Start by expressing your genuine interest in their platform or event and highlight how your expertise aligns with their content.

Share a brief overview of your background and what unique insights you can offer. Make it clear that you're open to tailoring your presentation or discussion to suit their audience's needs. Perhaps they would like someone to come and share a 10min presentation on 5 Top Tips For Starting Out as A Property Entrepreneur?

Or if you don't yet feel confident to cover that just yet, what about offering to share 5 Important Market Updates from the previous week / month on a regular basis. Just research and compile a list and share them at each event. That doesn't require any specific knowledge as you're just sharing other people's resources. Express your enthusiasm for collaborating and inquire about the possibility of helping their platform.

We run and host a number of local networking events and "Club Nights" as part of the Property Entrepreneurs Club. These range from a handful of people meeting up for a beer, to rooms of property professionals in a more formal, training setting. We actively promote and support our members to take to the stage and become accustomed to public speaking. These are a great way to get used to speaking in a safe and non-judgemental environment so come along to one of our next events to try them out.

Why not take the leap?

Remember, when you next hear about a speaking engagement or a podcast opportunity, consider the profound impact it can have on your property business. It's not just about sharing information — it's about positioning yourself as that credible professional, expanding your reach, and ultimately, driving your property business forward.

Awards & Features

Winning awards and being featured in recognised media outlets as a property entrepreneur is like getting a big thumbs-up from the industry. It's not just about having a shiny trophy on your shelf, or kudus for being featured - it's about what that trophy and feature represents.

When you win an award, it's a sign that your hard work, dedication, and innovative ideas are being recognised by experts in the field. There are many kinds of awards to choose from: national, local, even industry-based. Each of these offer a platform to showcase your accomplishments to a wider audience, which can lead to increased brand recognition and business opportunities. As an award winner, you stand out in a crowded market, positioning yourself as a standout choice among competitors.

Awards and features also serve as valuable networking tools. Industry events where awards are presented provide opportunities to connect with fellow entrepreneurs, investors, and key players in the property sector. These connections can lead to partnerships, collaborations, and access to new markets.

Begin by researching awards and publications or media outlets that specifically cater to startups or emerging entrepreneurs in the property sector. Once you identify suitable awards and outlets, carefully review their criteria and submission guidelines. Prepare a compelling application that highlights your achievements, unique approach, and the value you bring to the industry.

Be sure to emphasise your growth trajectory and any notable accomplishments that showcase your potential. Craft an impactful narrative that demonstrates your dedication to the property field.

Winning awards and becoming featured can be a very smart move that can really help your personal brand and property business stand out and obtain quick traction, especially when you're starting out.

My businesses utilise the support of a PR company who puts us in front of certain media outlets and also submits us for awards. So we outsource much of this effort which pays back 10 fold.

Start Now

Every single person who reads this book has more knowledge, experience and skills which can be leveraged to start building credibility than they probably realise. This is why we start by mapping out all of our existing skills, knowledge, experiences, resources, network etc. You should've done this already by this stage - refer to Chapter 2. These are the pillars we can build from and begin to leverage.

Starting now, crafting your brand and increasing your visibility as a property entrepreneur is going to massively help get your business in front of clients, investors, agents, and everyone who wants to work with you.

While you may not see immediate results, the effort you invest in today will undoubtedly pave the way for long-term trust and success in your property business.

PART 5
PROSPECT

CHAPTER 9

ATTRACTING DEALS THROUGH AGENTS

In this chapter, we're going to discuss your not-so-secret weapon for finding property opportunities and deals – yet many people get this totally wrong – and that's converting local estate agents into your very own personalised sourcing agents.

If you're the type who is reading this thinking that this sounds too good to be true, trust me – it's a real thing that actually happens! They'll send all the good stuff straight to your inbox, often before it hits the open market.

If you're the type who is reading this thinking you've heard it all before then yes I admit, this isn't anything new or groundbreaking. But what astounds me is the number of people who over complicate things and try to conjure up new, creative ways for finding deals when really, all the answers are right in front of their faces.

Personally the vast majority of my property deals have been done via agents, and over the years I've turned multiple estate agents into sourcing agents who bring me deals directly and it works like a charm.

Only a short while back I received a WhatsApp message out of the blue from one of my agent contacts. I had met him a year or so prior at a local networking event, built some rapport and learnt that he liked his golf. I treated him to a round at my local course a few weeks prior to receiving the message so I was clearly front of mind.

This message didn't say anything except a random address followed by four walkthrough videos. I rang him straight away and he told me he'd literally just jumped in the car having visited this property. He said it's a probate, low lease and they want £125k for it. But with a little refurb it'll easily be worth £180k plus.

I said great, give me half an hour and I'll come back to you.

29 mins later I messaged him back asking if they would take a £120k cash buy and if so, you've got a buyer. After a few more messages back and forth and a little chat

about what his fee was, we had the deal wrapped up at £125k. The deal included a brand new lease and his company gets tenancy management for a min of two years.

Here are the numbers…

Purchase	**£125,000 Inc a new 125yr lease**
Legals & SDLT	**£4,000**
Refurb & Costs	**£18,000**
Total Costs	**£147,000**
Re-valuation after 6 months	**£180,000**
Money out via 75% LTV mortgage	**£135,000**
Money Left In after all remortgage costs	**£12,000**
Net Rent per annum after agent fees	**£9,600**
Return on Capital Employed	**80%**

As you can see, a nice little deal. All directly from a local estate agent.

In this section of the book, I'm going to take you through why agents would even entertain working with you in the first instance, and give you some tips and tricks to make deals just like this, drop into your lap. But of course, this chapter goes hand in hand with the previous because it relies on knowing how to position and promote yourself.

What's In It For Them?

Let's get this one dealt with straight off the bat. I know you might be wondering, why would estate agents send you deals directly instead of going through the open market? Why bother sending a deal to just one person when they could access multiple potential buyers via the open market?

The answer is simple – when an agent sends a deal directly to an investor like me or you, they already know what they're going to get - and that is a higher chance of a sale. Assuming we have positioned ourselves well, they will know that we, as investors, are in a good position to act fast on the sale, and will do what we say we will.

Statistics show that around 1-in-3 sales agreed fall through before completion and often that is due to buyers messing sellers around, having financial issues or playing silly buggers at the 9th hour.

Not only does an agent benefit from a more likely sale, by coming to you or I, but they also get an easy sale too. Instead of going through the hassle of marketing the property to a wide range of buyers, making the listing look all pretty, uploading it and going through all that process - they can simply reach out to a few ready-to-go developers or investors like us. It saves them time, effort, and money that they would otherwise have to spend on marketing.

Working with investors directly means that agents don't have to onboard new clients and conduct various checks, like proof of funds or anti-money laundering checks. If they already have a shortlist of investors who they know are already good to go, it's much quicker and easier for them.

Finding An Agent

So where can you find an agent that you can turn into your sourcing agent? Well, there are a number of ways to connect with agents, but of course it is the type of agents that you are looking for.

A. Property networking events

I have found over the years that the type of agents who are keen to build these types of relationships and work with you, have an understanding of the investor market. They will often attend or sponsor local property networking events.

This gives further reason for attending these events and utilising your positioning and promotional skills. Focus on building rapport and credibility with them - they're interested in whether you are proceedable, and whether you will deliver on what you say.

B. Go on viewings

In the past I have found a few potential deals that are along the lines of what we are looking for as a business and despite them not being quite right, I have still booked in viewings with the sole purpose of meeting the agent.

C. Independent agents can be best

When approaching agents, focus on independents or those who are part of smaller chains. Usually these type of agency set ups are more flexible in the way they do things and are more open to being more creative with you. Agents from larger corporate agencies generally have stricter guidelines and processes due to their structure. You may still find a few agents within those agencies who are willing to work with you, but usually it heeds fewer results.

D. Agents who preferably want to invest for themselves

Agents who already invest for themselves are unlikely to send you all the good deals, but agents who want to start investing are perfect. They understand both sides of the coin and may also be seeking potential support from an investor like you to guide them through the process. They may also be willing to collaborate, partner up on deals and be able to bring certain skill sets to the table.

What To Do When Speaking With Agents

1. Build rapport

It's important to remember that in the property business, it's all about person-to-person connections, even though a lot of things are now done online. So if you want to turn your estate agent into a sourcing agent, you have to build rapport with them first. You can't just waltz into their office and demand deals without building or establishing any relationship. It's give-and-take.

So here are a few things you can do to build rapport with estate agents.

a. Pick one contact

You can choose one specific person within the agency to focus on building a strong relationship with. Ideally you want it to be a sales negotiator, a branch manager, or even better, the owner. These are the people who have the most extensive networks and are out there actively finding deals as their commission relies on getting deals over the line.

b. Invest time & energy

Invest your time and energy into nurturing the relationship. Think of it as if you're dating. Don't try too hard or come across desperate. Be sincere with your approach and take the time to get to know them as a person. This is also why networking events can work really well as you have a preset environment to spend time together and get to know them on a personal level. Find out what they like and drop in "oh we should go for a round of golf soon" or if they're into their coffee say "have you heard of this coffee place that does the best lattes, I'll treat you if you fancy?" If they're into their sports, find out their favourite football team or sportsperson, bring it up in conversation next time you see them. These little things help build rapport, strengthen the bond and start opening doors.

c. Be concise, be you

Another important point is to be concise and honest about what you're doing and what business you're building. Clearly communicate that you're a property entrepreneur seeking specific types of deals. Remember, agents appreciate people who are direct and don't beat around the bush because they will expect the same approach to play out when you get one of their deals into conveyancing.

d. Don't drop off their radar

Stay on their radar. If you build a relationship with an agent, make sure you follow up and keep in touch. They might not have deals for you right away, but you want to be at the forefront of their minds when they do come across something suitable. Send them a quick text or email every few weeks to check in to see how business is going and to ask if they've got anything interesting. It will maintain the relationship but also show them that you're serious about getting something tied up.

e. Give them something back

Remember, relationships are give and take so try to put yourself in the agent's shoes and think about what they would want from someone like you. Perhaps you can help them expand their network by introducing finance brokers, a good solicitor or someone who could bring value to their business. Better still, if you have heard about someone wanting to sell their house, give your agent their number and the inside track.

2. Build credibility

Apart from establishing that human connection with your agents, it's also important to keep building your credibility. Credibility is important because this allows you to be seen as someone amicable, yet professional – it shows that you're dependable and crucially are in a strong position to pull the trigger!

a. Always respond to their messages and communications

If they send you a deal or put you on their mailing list, even if it's not relevant to you, respond and give them feedback. If they leave a voicemail, make sure you return the call and apologise for missing it. Being responsive shows that you're reliable, which helps build that credibility.

b. Do what you say

When you say you'll do something, follow through on it. If you promise to call them next week or review a potential lead, make sure you do it. Keep your word and take action. It's crucial to build that trust by doing what you say you'll do.

c. **Tell them you work with clients**

Not only does this build credibility that you are not a lone ranger and are part of something bigger, but it also gives you a get out of jail free card in the event that they ask for proof of funds, or why you aren't the person who ends up buying the deal.

d. **Follow up on viewings**

After any viewing, ensure you follow up with feedback. Let them know if the property didn't meet your criteria or if it's of interest. Furthermore, I try to always make offers on the properties I view. Even if it's not perfect, you can just make a low ball offer and justify to the agent why. They'll start to see that you are business minded and that should be vendor accept, you have the creativity to extract value.

e. **Make offers & justify**

When making offers, don't shy away from explaining why you're offering that particular figure, or conditions. By providing justification, the agent, despite being employed by the vendor, will sometimes want to work with you to convince the vendor to go with you.

Fees

When it comes to fees, only ask about them if you're seriously considering a deal, because there's no point in asking about fees if you're not going to move forward. Most of the time, the vendor (property seller) will be responsible for paying the estate agent's fees, so even if the agent sends you the deal directly, their fees should already be covered by the vendor. However, if the fees haven't been clarified upfront, and you're interested in the deal, ask the agent who is responsible for paying the fees.

Now, even if the vendor is paying the fees, it's always a good gesture to offer to contribute something - especially if they are sending you the deal directly before it hits the open market. I usually include around 1% in my deal analysis as a sweetener to the deal and to maintain a good relationship with the agent. This way, if the agent mentions any issues with the vendor regarding fees, you've already factored it into your numbers.

If the agent doesn't ask for anything, or if you don't want to offer anything, then that extra 1% you've allowed for just becomes additional profit for you. If you end up successfully securing the deal, you can offer them a small amount as a token of appreciation. They may decline, but if they accept, it's a nice way to strengthen your relationship.

Remember, the fees are generally paid by the vendor, so it's not something you need to overcomplicate. However, if it's not clear, wait until you find a deal before discussing fees with agents.

What if?

By this point, hopefully it's getting clear on how you can begin approaching an agent to send you deals directly but in case there's a few "what-ifs" going through your head. Let's run through a few that might be bothering you.

"What if I don't have any clients?"

There might be some of you who've read through this chapter with one question reverberating in your head: "but Tanner, I don't have any clients". Just because you don't have any clients now doesn't mean you won't have them when the time comes! Don't overthink it – just focus on finding the deal first, and the money will follow. Remember The Deal Triangle™ from Chapter 7?

You'll do whatever it takes to get the money once you have a good deal in hand, so don't stress. If you spend time thinking about how you don't have any clients at this stage will only serve as a self-limiting belief, and that's the last thing you want right now. Have faith, stay determined, and believe in yourself. Once you've found the deal, I know you'll do absolutely whatever it takes to find the money and get the clients.

"What if I don't have proof of funds?"

Similarly, don't fret. If you don't have the funds or the required documentation to prove it to the agent, it comes down to how well you've built rapport and trust with them. If they specifically ask for proof of funds, there are always alternatives you can provide. You can speak to your mortgage broker and obtain an agreement in principle or a letter stating your financial position. Join a community or mastermind, or engage with a mentor who would be willing to help. Don't overthink it for now. Focus on finding the deal, and you can figure out the proof of funds later.

"What if I don't know who's buying it?"

What if you don't know if you're buying it in your own name, or under a limited company name, or in a partnership? What if you don't know how you'll finance it altogether?

Again, this is just a matter of crossing the bridge when you get there. The answer to these questions are steps six to eight, and right now, you have to concentrate on steps one to five, which involves building relationships with agents and finding good deals. Keep your options open when discussing the property. Mention that you work with clients or have a business partner.

This allows you to explore various avenues, such as partnering with someone or bringing in an investor, when the time comes to make a decision. Don't stress about the specifics just yet.

"What if I just don't have the confidence?"

If you haven't figured it out already, confidence plays a huge role in this process. If you feel unsure or lack belief in yourself, it's important to understand that this feeling is not serving you at all – it's just a limiting belief.

Remember, if I can do it, you can too! Don't let a lack of confidence hold you back. Reach out for support and guidance, whether it's from me or someone in your network and focus on building that confidence.

"What if I don't know enough?"

This is exactly the same as feeling like you're not confident enough – if I'm being honest, I think nobody knows enough, you just have to be confident that you are able to learn. Just the fact that you're here reading this book makes me believe that you have everything in you to be able to learn and do the best you can do.

The key here is to keep learning and gaining more knowledge. Get out there and view properties, even if you're not initially interested in them. Most importantly, don't be afraid to make those mistakes – mistakes will happen, but that's how we learn and grow.

Tips And Tricks Of Things To Say

When you want to position yourself to an agent, tell them these things:

"I work with clients and partners"

Informing agents that you collaborate with clients and partners, enhances your credibility and authority as a serious property professional - you're not just another Joe Bloggs looking to buy one property. It also helps you overcome the "proof of funds" hurdle that many newer property investors face.

By being upfront that you work with others provides you a get out of jail free card for when they ask for proof of funds, as you can send someone else's (with their permission of course!) Again if you are part of our mastermind, we can help here too.

"Money is not an issue"

Assure them that funding is readily available due to your clients' financial capacity. When asked about potential buyers, explain that decisions are made based on financial evaluation. Whether it's buying for clients or ourselves, the focus is on a profitable deal. This approach allows you to confidently make offers, secure acceptance, and plan the details afterward, demonstrating your reliability to them.

"I will get this completed"

Share with them that you're a person of action—when you commit, you follow through. So if an agent makes an offer, tell them that it's your commitment to see it through. Whether it's accepted immediately or requires further discussion, you should remind them that your intention is always completion.

Display that you hold the values that will ensure a successful deal closure. Plus as we've already established, you will only be making offers where deals will hit your metrics anyway.

"I need to speak to my business partner"

Another useful approach is to involve your business partner, whether you have one or not. If agents ask about immediate buying decisions or ask a question you don't know the answer to, you can reply that you need to confer with your business partner. You can just say "great question, I need to speak to my business partner and come back to you."

This allows you time to gather your thoughts, reach out for support and respond accordingly.

CHAPTER 10
FINDING DEALS USING WHAT ACTUALLY WORKS

Whilst much of what we have covered so far is aimed at positioning and promoting yourself to *attract* deals and opportunities, this chapter focuses on what you can do to proactively go out there and *find* deals.

Over the years many books, webinars and training courses have been sold (and many educators have made a lot of money doing so) covering different strategies one could use to market and find deals. I've tried many of these strategies and spent thousands on learning and implementing them. And I can tell you right now that most of them are utter hot air.

The next new strategy might sound great and creative, but quite often very little has been tried and tested. I don't know about you but I'm more interested in sharing what actually works and what is going to move the needle in the biggest, most cost effective way.

Fundamentally, what works best can be summarised into four things:

1. **Agents** - we've already covered this in Chapter 9 - but it's free.
2. **Portals** - it's how you use them and knowing what to look for - and they're free.
3. **Direct letters** - utilising a handful of resources to identify sites - this has a cost.
4. **Billboards/Bandit boards** - cheap as chips and highly effective.

Portals

Apart from agents, the ever-reliable World Wide Web can be a great source for numerous deals, if you know where to look. The key here is to identify what type of deals you are looking for and where. Then you can focus on utilising the portals to do much of legwork for you.

Online platforms such as Rightmove and Zoopla, are better for residential opportunities. Whereas platforms like EG Property Link are great for commercial property. There are also fancier tools such as Nimbus Maps and LandTech that enable you to locate specific plots of specific sizes. I love these tools and will cover these below in the "direct letters" section, as you are required to send out letters to the sites that you find using these tools.

While there is a notion that the *best* deals are off-market, that's not always the case. It is important to understand that a project needs to offer three elements in order to land in the "deal zone".

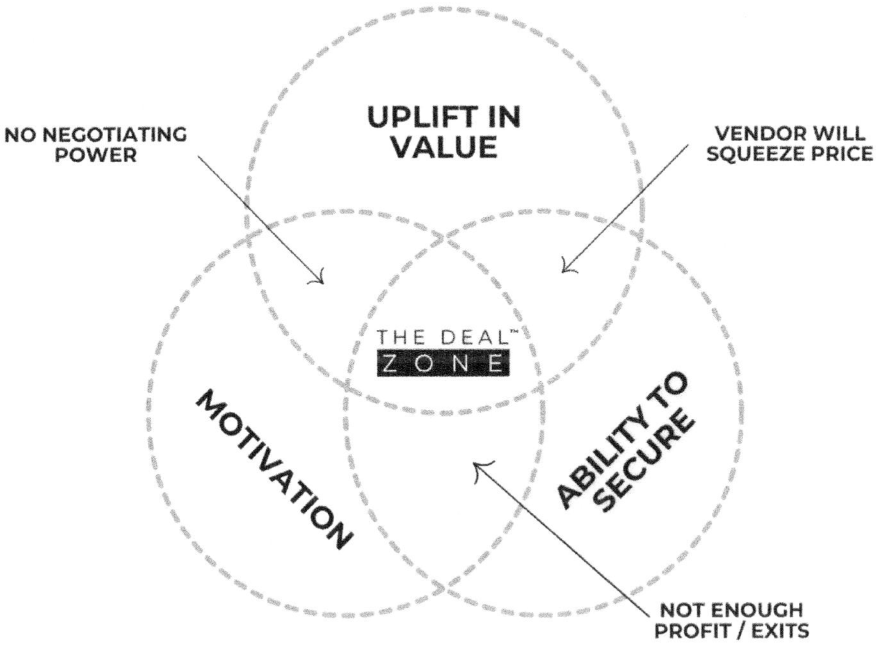

1. Enough scope for creating an **uplift in value** - no uplift in value, then highly unlikely to be enough profit in the deal, or have a decent exit.

2. **Motivation** from the vendor's side. Not enough motivation, then the vendor will squeeze the price. High motivation then the vendor will take an offer.
3. Your **ability to secure** the deal. If you are not in a position to complete, you will have lower negotiation power and you won't get it over the line.

So why is this relevant when talking about portals?

By knowing these three things, you can start to tailor your searches and set up alerts for properties and scenarios where the motivation is high and there is a good opportunity for uplift, whether that be via conversion, refurb, title splitting, development etc. Here are a number of ways you could now use the portals:

- Sorting listings by oldest shows a higher likelihood that **motivation** to sell is higher, or maybe there is a problem with the property and that could present an opportunity to negotiate a reduced price against asking.
- Identifying *Sold Subject To Contract* deals which have also been on market for a long time, particularly over 9-10 months may indicate a problem property that could be struggling to complete for numerous reasons, therefore it may be about to come back to market with a high

motivation to turn around quickly with a proceedable buyer.

- Searching for keywords such as "motivated", "refurbishment", "cash", "investor", or "plot" will usually churn out uplift opportunities. I have provided a list of the top 15 keywords to use in online portals at the back of this book.

You can also use portals to identify micro-areas within towns and cities where property prices are cheaper, and therefore where you can pick up properties more affordably. To do this follow these steps:

1. Search a chosen area (town, city etc).
2. Select a particular type of property (such as a 2 bed, terraced house).
3. Ensure filters such as New Homes, Retirement Homes and Shared Ownership are deselected (we're not interested in them).
4. Choose a max value (ideally one that will cover most properties in your area) and hit search.
5. Toggle on to map view - this will show where you can pick up 2 bed terraced houses within the budget you set.
6. Slowly decrease the maximum value - as you start to remove listings you'll be able to see where clusters form identifying lower value areas.

This same approach can be used to identify properties that are in higher value areas but are listed for cheap as they will be outliers. We have a training video walking you through these steps (amongst many others) as part of the Property Entrepreneurs Club Online Training portal - if you would like more information visit us at https://www.propertyentrepreneurs.club/dmd-book-resource.

When I first started in property I used these exact steps to identify my first investment area in Portsmouth, which I went on to buy multiple properties in. I created uplift and cashflow utilising the HMO strategy, and replaced my engineering salary within 2 short years. There are still so many untapped areas throughout the UK where strategies such as HMOs work so well. However I often see investors over thinking things and being scared to take forward steps and crack on with doing deals.

Using portals can not only help identify areas of opportunity, as well as deals themselves, but help with much of the due diligence too as the data is all there to hand. By using the same techniques you can identify what the ceiling price is for different types of properties in different areas.

Direct Letters

There's been much debate over the years as to how effective "old-school" mailouts actually are. With much of modern marketing moving online where practically everyone now has a smartphone I have actually found that the stats on old-school mail campaigns have improved. I suspect this is down to the fact that many people have moved online and given up on the letter drops, and there is less competition.

There are a few elements to making a successful direct mailing campaign. It's often less about the content of the letter, and more about finding a better source of leads.

In the UK my preferred source of leads is by far The Gazette - https://www.thegazette.co.uk/

The Gazette is a free public record and thus an excellent source of information. It lists a number of different things, but for us we are most interested in the following listings:

1. All notices of Wills & Probates
2. Business Insolvencies

The reason these two are of interest is because usually they come with property assets that need to be sold off as part of either the probate process or insolvency.

This means we can scrape data in our local areas and send letters to a very targeted set of leads. You can send letters to both the executors of the probates/insolvencies and to the properties/directors directly.

It is important to understand the situations, so wording the letters accordingly and sympathetically is important, however I have found over the years that this is an excellent source of motivated property leads. The best bit, it's completely free.

Head on over there and have a look around. I would recommend having four letter templates:

1. One for the executors of probates - usually solicitors
2. One to send directly to probate properties
3. One to send to administrators of insolvencies
4. One to send directly to directors addresses of insolvent companies

It is important to set yourself a budget to cover your marketing methods and ensure that you are re-sending letters to the same people. Just sending one letter isn't always enough to convince someone to pick up the phone and call. We like to send a letter at least four times to the same address over the course of six months.

Billboards / Bandit Boards

Utilising billboards and what we refer to as "bandit boards" are always a highly effective way to access opportunities directly "on patch".

Billboards are more expensive and are usually secured via a provider. Whereas bandit boards are those small "We Buy Any House" style boards that you sometimes see attached to lamp posts and the like.

Whilst most councils don't like you using bandit boards, and you have to be prepared to take a wrap to the knuckles, they can be highly effective.

I received a phone call one day from a chap who had seen one of our boards. He was in some financial difficulty and had a commercial unit that he was looking to sell. We took some details, did a bit of research and agreed to a meeting on site. I visited him, built some rapport and made an offer to solve his problem. His business had failed a couple of years ago - which operated out of his commercial unit.

He had kept hold of the unit until now and was emotionally attached to it; however he now needed some quick cash to pay off a few debts that had been mounting.

I agreed to buy his unit from him for £78,500 in cash and would complete within six weeks. We did a light refurb and found a local tenant who secured it from us on a five year FRI (Fully Repairing and Insuring) Lease.

These were the headline figures:

Purchase	**£78,500 Inc new 199yr lease**
Legals & SDLT	**£600**
Refurb & Costs	**£8,000**
Gross Cost	**£87,100**
Net Rent p.a	**£12,000**
Gross Yield	**13.8%**

Now at the time of writing we have decided to leave this unit unencumbered, generating a 13.8% ROCE. However we could at some point in the future look to raise finance against this unit as follows:

Revaluation @ 9% Yield	**£135,000**
Money Out @ 70% LTV	**£94,500**
Money Left In Deal	**£0** Assuming a few thousand in refinance costs
Net Rent p.a	**£9,000**
R.O.C.E	**INFINITE**

This deal was secured directly from a £7.48 bandit board.

PART 6
PERSIST

CHAPTER 11
TRACKING LEADS AND FOLLOWING UP

We make it to our final stage of the Do More Deals Framework™ - the last piece of the puzzle that completes the picture. This stage is all about not giving up, because one thing I have learnt in the years I have had on this planet is that usually the most persistent people are the most successful.

In order to generate consistent returns for you and your business, you have to put in consistent effort. Let me bring you back to the lake analogy I shared right at the beginning of this book. A big reason for why many people do not succeed is their lack of persistence and focus. The shiny penny syndrome. Or they try it once and then give up.

Success is the sum of small efforts, repeated day-in, day-out. Therefore I would like to share with you a few crucial aspects to property that will help you see more consistent results.

The Easy AS…F Method

The Easy AS…F Method is pretty straight forward but often, as I've mentioned many times throughout this book, people massively over complicate things when they need not. They think they are being smart by trying new things but really these next three steps are as complicated as it needs to get.

So what does the Easy AS…F Method mean? Well, AS…F means:

1. Act Fast
2. Systemise
3. Follow the Fuck Up!

Let's break these down a little.

1. Act Fast

Picture this: you've got a decision to make and you're like, "Hmm, let me sleep on it" or "Let me just speak to so-and-so"…

Well, in the property *and* in business, speed is often key - and it is key for two reasons.

One: If someone tosses you a sweet opportunity or deal, the last thing you want to do is to let it simmer for five days, because while you're pondering, either someone else might swoop in like a hawk and snag it, or whoever sent it to you in the first instance will just think you're not serious and just another one of those tire-kickers.

Two: The longer it takes to make a decision, the decision gets bigger in your mind. It just ratchets up the pressure to make the decision.

The key here is getting comfortable making quick decisions, even if the outcomes don't always go your way. Trust me, the speed of your moves count big time. Hesitate too much, and the opportunity might just vanish. It may be uncomfortable at first but you soon get more comfortable in those moments. If you are the type of person who struggles to make decisions then identify this fact, own it and get some help. That's where a good mentor, coach or peer group can massively help in seeing things objectively and removing a lot of the emotion.

I remember being introduced to this potential deal a number of years back. It was a large commercial development site right next to a mainline train station which had huge potential. It was all very exciting, I was in direct contact with the vendor who was an uncle of one of my friends. I went to visit the site, and met with the owner. We built great rapport and I went away from the site viewing with the promise that I would get back to him within the week. However I just dwelled on it. Other things cropped up during the week, I hit some kind of paralysis.

Four days passed and the back of my head was saying I need to make a decision on what to do here. Then another few days passed and I just could not decide what to do. Over a week passed and I didn't know what to go back to the vendor with. The need to make a decision, any decision just grew in my head and it started to consume my thoughts. I started to struggle sleeping, always thinking about this deal and the fact I hadn't gone back to the vendor when I said I would. It was not a nice feeling. In the end, I emailed the vendor and just said that I was unable to proceed with the deal. I didn't give specifics but by just making a decision enabled me to move on and focus on other things.

In hindsight, the deal was too big for me at that moment in my career, however rather than own that fact, and go back to the vendor sooner to say it wasn't for me, my ego got in the way. I had this massive opportunity for which I was in pole position for, yet I froze, allowed it to consume me and meant all the other important tasks that needed doing at the time were also forgotten. However this taught me a few lessons; firstly that when faced with a difficult decision, always share it and seek advice. That Lone Wolf approach just doesn't serve you when someone else may have been able to help structure something you don't yet know about.

Secondly, just making any decision frees up the mind and allows you to move forward. Trying to hold on to everything at all times and maximise every opportunity can actually have a negative impact on your progress. So get comfortable being uncomfortable, make quicker decisions and rather than be afraid of regretting them, learn from them.

2. Systemise

Now, it might be a bit of an adrenaline rush looking at all the potential deals out there, but don't forget – this isn't a hobby, it's a business. So you want to be mindful of systems – those nifty little tools that make everything click and automate many aspects. The more you weave systems into your processes, the more you can do, and the sooner you can move on to building a team.

Initially you need to identify which type of systems you need based upon which type of processes and tasks that are being done in your business. The most obvious process when looking to build a property investment business is finding and tracking opportunities.

Using CRM To Track Deals

There are two popular CRMs we use to track opportunities: Podio and Trello. Although there are hundreds available on the market. We use Podio as it's cheap and highly adaptable. You can do a lot of cool things with it and systemise and automate a lot of workflows. It's also a good tool for team management and communication.

Trello, on the other hand, is completely free but as you would expect, its functionality is more limited. It's up to you to identify what processes you need to track and find a solution that suits your needs best. Regardless of whichever CRM you end up using, the key priority is you want to systemise processes as much as possible. You don't want to waste time on tedious admin tasks, or sifting through reams of paper for that phone number of a vendor you spoke to six months ago.

A CRM will help you manage your leads a lot better, build a team so you can focus on higher-income generating tasks but also allows you to hand responsibilities over to others easier.

But here's the real gem: follow-up.

3. Follow The Fuck Up!

When you have a CRM in place, you can get better at following up on opportunities. As we discussed in the previous chapter, motivation is a key component to finding good deals. However a large percentage of property investors make an offer on a property, have it rejected and then move on. They never circle back round. Most would tell the agent, "well, here's the offer, let me know if it's still on the market".

The thing is, most agents won't come back to you unless you remind them – nine times out of ten, the agent is probably going to forget to come back to you. That's why having a system in place to schedule a follow up is crucial. I always set reminders to reach out again after four weeks, eight weeks and six months. If the property still hasn't been sold, your initial offer may start looking a bit more attractive.

A few years ago we completed this deal. I saw the property on Rightmove in the October time listed for £160,000. I contacted the agent and they said the deal was under offer. I diarised to follow up with them a few weeks later. Which I did, and still under offer.

In the meantime the values in the local area were visibly going up. We made an offer on a smaller property a few roads down for £155k which was accepted. Then a few months down the line I had a notification in my diary to follow up with the agent again on the first one. I rung them and they said "Good timing, we were just informed this morning that the other buyers can no longer complete and so the property is now available. We were about to re-list it online."

I made an offer to purchase the property there and then at £160,000 as I knew the true market value for it was around the £190,000 mark. It was agreed, we completed within a few months and within nine months we flipped it back on the open market for £225,000. After all costs we made around £30,000 profit from that deal all because I systemised and scheduled a follow up call - and actually followed the fuck up. That phone call was worth £30k!

So, remember, follow-up is the name of the game. It's the one thing you should always do when it comes to property and sourcing deals. Don't hesitate to make an offer and then follow up consistently. Trust me, the biggest deals often come from this alone.

So, there you have it – the ASF method:
Act Fast, Systemise, Follow the Fuck Up.

CONCLUSION

Growing a property business is more than just a side hustle; it's a proper commitment. Sure, there are challenges, but the rewards are HUGE.

In the pages of this book, I've guided you through the Do More Deals Framework™—my comprehensive six-part approach that began with cultivating a growth mindset to having the skills to manage your consistent flow of deals efficiently.

We've explored the aspects of developing a Deal Makers Mindset, crafting a thorough plan, leveraging your strengths, strategies to enhance your visibility, effective methods for discovering good deals, and ensuring successful closures.

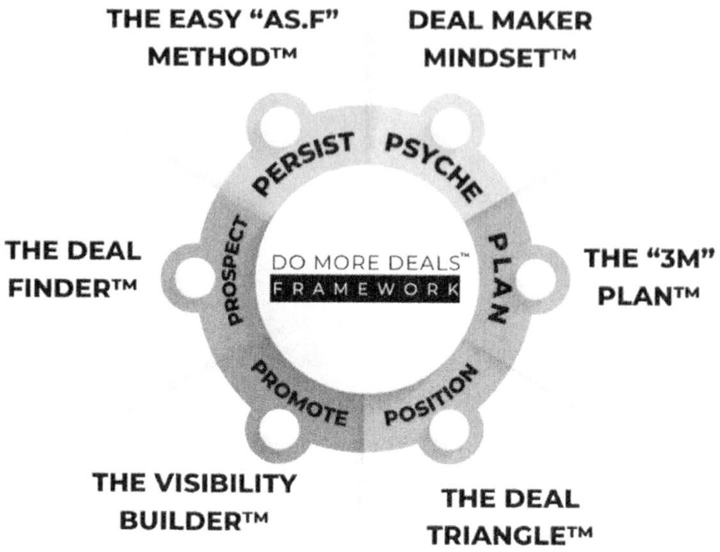

Always remember, building your property business is more than just getting another deal; it turns you into someone who plans out how to generate income and sets up financial freedom to be able to have the resources to do what is most important to you.

There might be a part of you that thinks growing your property business is a massive undertaking and almost feels impossible.

But the most exciting aspect is that you now have a clear set of steps to follow, providing you with a reliable guide along the way.

By following the well-organised framework, you'll consistently have established strategies to refer back to as you navigate through the stages of your growth.

Whether you're just starting out, competing in the proverbial business marathon or just looking to maximise on your potential, this book ensures you stay on track and avoid getting lost in the process.

Truth be told, building your property business from the ground up can lead to all kinds of challenges, including acquiring additional skills, financial obstacles, and complexities of deal negotiations. My hope is that, through reading this book, you've gained valuable insights on overcoming these challenges and more.

But keep in mind that during one of the most turbulent periods in the UK property sector, there is massive opportunity. Whilst many are on the brink of financial struggle, others are on the edge of substantial growth, and I genuinely hope you'll be among the latter. When there is increased uncertainty, there is increased opportunity.

So, if you're committed to building a successful property business, when that is via building a portfolio, becoming a property developer or scaling a serviced based business then ensure you follow the steps we cover within this book.

How you think, how you plan, how you position yourself, what you say, how you promote yourself and what you do to move the needle is all going to have a material impact on how quickly you achieve the goals that you set for yourself.

One thing is for certain, success and failure are completely predictable. I have had the pleasure to work with hundreds of people within the property sector who have transformed their businesses and personal lives by Doing More Deals.

If you haven't done so yet, access the extra resources that complement the content in this book at https://www.propertyentrepreneurs.club/dmd-book-resource. Discover more about how I could assist you in developing your property business and doing more deals.

Remember, taking action involves risks and costs, but they are significantly lower than the long-term risks and costs of staying where you are now.

I appreciate you for taking the time to read this book and I wish you all the success and prosperity on your future endeavours.

APPENDIX

Top 15 Keywords for Online Portals:

1. Reduced
2. Motivated
3. Refurbishment
4. Cash (just the singular as this picks up cash-buyers, cash-buy, cash-only etc)
5. Quick Sale
6. Investor (just the singular as this picks up suit-an-investor, btl-investors etc)
7. Landlord
8. Plot (just the singular as this picks up building-plot, side-plot, development-plot etc)
9. Cosmetic updating
10. Modernisation
11. Chain (just the singular as this picks up chain-free as well as no-chain)
12. Development potential
13. Short lease
14. Relocating
15. Priced To Sell